No limits!

FROM STUCK TO LIMITLESS

A COLLECTION OF INSPIRING ESSAYS THAT WILL CHANGE YOUR LIFE AND MINDSET

MARIE MCKENZIE **ERIC JONES, JR.**
JULAINE ROBINSON **MINDI FETTERMAN**
MARVA RILEY **BRIDGETT RENAY**
SOLSIRÉ E. FELIDA **PATTY HARRIS** **J.L. CAMPBELL**
DR. VANESSA HOWARD **PAT G'ORGE-WALKER**
ANN WOOTEN-TAYLOR **VERONICA NEALY-MORRIS**

Marie McKenzie

MARIE L. MCKENZIE, LLC

From Stuck to limitless Copyright ©2023

ISBN: [eBook] 978-1-7371023-8-0

ISBN: [Trade Paperback] 978-1-7371023-9-7

Marie L. McKenzie LLC

Content Warning: This book, although not graphic, includes essays from individuals who discuss their experiences with PTSD, child abuse, and sexual assault.

This anthology is the work of non-fiction. Each essay is from the author's perspective and memories and is as accurate as possible.

Without limiting the rights under copyright reserved above, no part of this publication may be reproduced, stored in, or introduced into a retrieval system, or transmitted, in any form, or by any means (electronic, mechanical, photocopying, recording, or otherwise) without the express written permission of both the copyright owner and the publisher of this book, except in the case of brief quotations embodied in critical articles and reviews.

For permission, contact Marie McKenzie at marielmckenzie@gmail.com or at www.marielmckenzie.com

The scanning, uploading, and distribution of this book via the Internet or via any other means without the permission of the owner is illegal and punishable by law. Please purchase only authorized electronic editions and do not participate in or encourage electronic piracy of copyrighted materials. Your support of the author's rights is appreciated.

Marie McKenzie, et al: From Stuck to Limitless. Marie L McKenzie LLC.

If you purchase this book without a cover, you should be aware that this book is stolen property. It is reported as "unsold and destroyed" to the publisher, and neither the author nor the publisher has received any payment for this "stripped" book.

All Scripture quotations are taken from the following:

The King James Version / New King James Version®. Copyright © 1982 by Thomas Nelson

Life Application Study Bible, 1996, New Living Translation by Tyndale House Publishers

Used by permission. All rights reserved.

Cover design & Editing J.L. Campbell - www.joycampbell.com

Beta Readers:

Veronica Nealy-Morris - veronicanealy@yahoo.com

Julaine K. Robinson - juleskbr@gmail.com

Solsire E. Felida - se-felida@hotmail.com

CONTENTS

Introduction	v
Acknowledgment	1
Foreword	2
Content Warning	3
Eric	5
1. Operation Enduring Freedom	6
About Eric Jones, Jr	11
Julaine	13
2. Path to Purpose	14
About Julaine Robinson	20
Mindi	23
3. "Saucy"	25
About Mindi Fetterman	30
Marva	33
4. No Health … No Wealth	34
About Marva Riley	40
Bridgett	43
5. I've Been Called Worse	44
About Bridgett Renay	49
Solsiré	51
6. Growing Up Broken	52
About Solsiré E. Felida	60
Patty	63
7. Post Traumatic Growth	64
About Pastor Patty Harris	71
Books by Pastor Patty:	73
J.L.	75
8. Healing the Hurt: Breaking Unhealthy Behavioral Patterns	77
About J.L. Campbell	86
Vanessa	87
9. Soulful Sounds from a Once Broken Spirit	88
About Dr. Vanessa Howard	95
Pat	97
10. On Broken Pieces	98
About Pat G'Orge-Walker	107

Ann	109
11. Exodus from the Wilderness of Obesity to Claim the Promised Land of Healthy and Fit for Life	110
About Ann Wooten-Taylor	116
Veronica	119
12. My Father's Touch	120
About Veronica Nealy-Morris	127
Marie	129
13. Joy Comes in the Morning	130
About Marie McKenzie	137
Practicing Mindfulness	139
Resources	141

INTRODUCTION

At the start of this project, I thought of including only women who have survived childhood sexual trauma and were now using their voices and purpose to serve others who were similarly affected. However, after seeking the Lord's guidance, I was led to incorporate those who have struggled with various adversities, sought and achieved healing, and are now doing their part to impact the lives of others.

"Healing yourself is connected with healing others." - Yoko Ono

According to Galatians 6:2, we should bear one another's burdens.

This anthology shares the stories of thirteen phenomenal individuals, twelve women and one man, who are change-makers and fire starters in their own unique way, by providing insights into their life journey to help you uplevel your life *From Stuck to Limitless*.

Many men and women have suffered traumatic experiences, some during childhood and others as adults. Whether it be sexual, mental, or physical abuse, neglect by parents, diet and health issues, or unfortunate circumstances that have disrupted their life and left them stuck. Any of the above can lead to a life of struggles, pain, and unfulfilled dreams and potential.

vi INTRODUCTION

If they are fortunate, like me, "the village" will jump in and offer help and resources that will change the trajectory of their lives and help to restore hope and faith in themselves and in humanity. According to the African proverb, "It takes a village to raise a child," which means a child's development may require the contribution of the whole community to ensure health and safety. Sometimes, even adults need "the village" to help them heal, grow, survive, and thrive. However, at times, all we need is one person to believe in us and offer a hand to help us improve our lives and walk in purpose.

My prayer is that this book will inspire, motivate, and give readers hope, that they too can survive and thrive no matter what the circumstances.

From Stuck to Limitless is not intended to diagnose or treat any mental or other conditions. This book is to encourage those who may have similar experiences, to bring awareness that they're not alone, and healing is possible.

Don't be distracted by, or focused on, your current situation. Be encouraged and shift your mindset to what is possible and reclaim your Joy.

Marie L. McKenzie
Visionary Author

ACKNOWLEDGMENT

FIRST, glory and honor to my Lord and Savior, for bringing me through. Special thanks to my husband, George, for his love and unwavering support in all I do.

To my brother, O'Keile, Aunt Herma, other family members and friends who have stood by me with prayers, words of encouragement, and support for my work.

To the "village", my twelve co-authors, who worked tirelessly with me to make this project a success.

Special thanks to J.L. Campbell, she was the factotum in this project —cover design, interior design, and editor—smoothed the edges in all areas and helped to unfold an amazing product.

Special thanks to Naleighna Kai, without whom my literary journey may not have started. Thank you for the supportive advice and encouragement.

To The Tribe Called Success for the incredible support throughout my writing journey. You all inspire me.

To those I did not mention by name and may have forgotten, thank you for all the love and encouragement. May your light never dim and your cup run over into your saucer.

FOREWORD

FIVE STARS for the new Anthology, *From Stuck to Limitless*, brainchild of Marie McKenzie, award-winning writer, who deftly shepherded this literary project that examines the changes in the lives of the thirteen writers involved, and will touch the lives of so many others who read their stories.

From Stuck to Limitless is an anthology featuring individuals who share their harsh truths of trauma, and survival—from childhood sexual and mental abuse, adult traumas, or debilitating health issues.

It is through such truth-telling that we learn we are not alone and that it is only through sharing that we can heal ourselves and give hope to others. Most moving is that each of these writers has found a way to use their renewed strength to heal others. They have become the "village," that may have failed them at a time they most needed it.

Thank you, Marie McKenzie, for perfecting the art of communal storytelling. Thank you to each of these brave truthtellers for sharing their stories. Your book gives truth to, "We are the Savior we've been waiting for."

Janis F. Kearney,
   Presidential biographer, memoirist,
   international speaker, writing teacher
   https://www.janisfkearney.com

CONTENT WARNING

Content Warning: This book, although not graphic, includes essays from individuals who discuss their experiences with PTSD, child abuse, and sexual assault, which may be triggering for some.

ERIC

The impact of *Operation Enduring Freedom* on the mental health of young soldiers cannot be overstated. For many, the experience of combat and exposure to life-threatening situations can lead to long-lasting trauma and psychological distress. While the campaign involved a variety of approaches, including military operations, diplomacy, and humanitarian aid efforts, the human cost of the conflict cannot be ignored.

Many soldiers who served in Operation Enduring Freedom returned home with physical injuries and mental health conditions, such as post-traumatic stress disorder (PTSD), depression, and anxiety.

The challenges of reintegrating into civilian life and dealing with the effects of trauma can be overwhelming, and many veterans struggle to find the support and resources they need to cope.

Fortunately, there are professionals who specialize in helping veterans and active-duty military personnel manage their mental health and recover from the effects of trauma. By partnering with a mental health professional, individuals can work through the challenges of combat-related stress and develop strategies for moving forward with their lives.

CHAPTER 1
OPERATION ENDURING FREEDOM

FIVE MONTHS after graduating from high school, I enlisted from Birmingham, Alabama into the United States Army in October of 2012. Being a young adult, this was a new and unnerving experience for me. As Private Eric Jones Jr., I chose to fight for my country at such a young age, not knowing what to expect in the future.

I started basic training on November 14th, 2012, at Fort Sill, Oklahoma, and was one in a class of two hundred and thirty soldiers. By the time we graduated from basic training, the class had decreased by forty-five, due to some recruits not being able to handle the intensity of the progression we had to endure.

At the end of basic training, every soldier was sent to advanced individual training (AIT), where each person learned the requirements and skills needed for the jobs they chose when they enlisted at the recruiting station. Upon completion of AIT, we were sent to our first duty station where our army career began. I started my duties on April 13th, 2013 in Fort Campbell, Kentucky. After I was processed, I met a soldier named Devin White, who later became my best friend. We instantly connected because we were both from the south and had many things in common.

In the army you have battle buddies, who in other words, are very close friends you work with, go to lunch with, and do everything else with. As a result, it's easy to get close to someone you see every day and in whose company you spend your whole work day.

After almost a month, both of us were told that our names were on the manifest for deployment and we needed to prepare to leave for Afghanistan. Now, when you put this into perspective, deployments in the military are nine months long. We were nineteen years old and eleven months removed from being high school seniors. Now, we were being shipped to a combat zone to risk our lives fighting for our country. It's crazy how quickly the tables can turn and your life changes.

When we first landed in Afghanistan we were nervous, of course, because we didn't know what to expect. Devin and I knew to trust our training and follow the instructions of our leadership. Our deployment was normal, compared to the average. During the first eight months in the country, there were a couple of casualties, but nothing too crazy to send us into panic mode.

Then, I will never forget the day we went on a mission in a village and my life changed forever. Devin and I were like brothers. We ate all our meals together, played cards together, and talked to each other's family members. We were like real-life brothers, blood or better, in some cases. We couldn't have been closer, our relationship was tight.

I remembered entering that village and getting into one of the worst shootouts in my army career. We lost half our team, including my best friend, Devin, who was killed beside me in combat. The military teaches you, in highly intense moments, to engage with the enemy until you have the upper hand and then look after the casualties. This is called 'care under fire' in the military.

We were in a firefight for twenty minutes, and my life flashed before my eyes. I thought I was going to die because we weren't getting any reinforcements to assist us. Finally, another unit came and helped us. But all I could see afterward was my best friend laying there lifeless, and my thoughts were on repeat. *My brother is gone. How am I going to break this to his family?*

Astonishingly, this happened thirty days before we were supposed to return home to the United States, which made the situation worse. We were almost home to our loved ones, and my friend and the rest of our brothers weren't so lucky and were taken out in combat.

The following month after we flew back to the United States to Fort Campbell, Devin's family contacted me and asked me to speak at his funeral. I had already planned on attending, but was surprised they asked me to speak. That was, by far, the hardest thing I've had to do. I was a nineteen-year-old combat veteran who experienced his first year of the military, including real combat situations, and lost my best friend. Who would have known or even thought that was how my first year of military life would be?

I attended the funeral in my dress blue uniform and spoke in front of three hundred people. Devin was a beloved person in our unit and his family, so, many people came to pay their respect. My speech was about how close we were and the last weeks of his life leading up to the tragic incident that caused his death in Afghanistan.

Shortly after the funeral and returning to work, I descended into a deep depression. In the military, at that time, it was frowned upon for someone to seek help for their mental health. The leadership looked at you as being weak, or trying to get out of your duties. However, I had gotten to a point where I wouldn't allow the words or opinions of other people to stop me from getting the help and support I needed to get my mental health back together. Especially after all the things I had experienced in the last ten months.

I became so depressed that I stopped doing things that once brought me joy, like going to bars, playing basketball, or hanging out with the guys. My life was confined to going from home to work and back, and remained that way for nearly one year. It was then I decided to seek professional help.

When I started going to behavioral health, my counselor, Tim Ellis, was an older white gentleman. I was skeptical at first, because this was new for me, and I had never shared my problems or my past experiences with anyone outside of my immediate family and friends. I had appointments with Ellis once a week in the afternoon for two years.

In the beginning, the conversations were really slow, but once I grew comfortable the sessions flowed very well. Sometimes, while at work, I'd remember I had a mental health appointment on certain days and looked forward to them. They became a big stress reliever. Ellis was a great counselor, and we developed a close relationship. He helped me through my depression week by week and although I'm retired from the military, I still talk to him to this day.

I know for sure that my decision to seek help and not get caught up in the military lifestyle was a big win for me. I'm happy I did because other soldiers in my unit that were in Afghanistan followed when they saw the results I had achieved through therapy.

Memorial Day will always be sad for me, even though the military recognizes all the fallen veterans that gave the ultimate sacrifice to our country. It reminds me that my friend, Devin, and I will never get the chance to tell those army stories to each other, as I do now with my other buddies who served with me. However, I'm appreciative of the time we got to spend together and know that God had bigger plans for him.

My depression stemmed from blaming myself for his death. On the day he passed, I had to choose between taking out a suicide bomber that could kill many people, or a sniper that could only shoot one round at a time.

Looking back at the incident and the clarity I gained through mental health treatment, it was a lose-lose situation. It was unfortunate that we all couldn't make it home to our loved ones in one piece. There were many times while in Afghanistan, that it could have been me that was in that casket. I thank God I lived and am able to tell the story.

That's why I started a podcast called "The Eric J The Great Podcast," to provide a space for us to have conversations among ourselves, and have reassurance that no matter how poor or rich a person is, we still go through similar struggles, especially mentally.

The experiences I had in the military, especially in combat situations and behavioral health to heal my mental state, made me into the man I am today. I'm thankful for everyone who played a part in helping me through the roughest part of my life mentally—the tragic loss of my best friend.

These situations made me a big advocate for behavioral health and that's why, no matter how big or how small the situation, I always tell people to talk to a professional. Mental health treatment is confidential. Therapists don't know the people in your life, so they can't tell your business to them. And even if they did, by law they cannot share without your consent. It's a safe place and sometimes that's all a person needs, a nonjudgmental safe zone to express their emotions about what they are going through.

Mental health will always be a priority in my life and I will continue to have my counselor close at hand. Whenever I go through a mental obstacle or feel overwhelmed, I reach out to my counselor and get the help and support I need. I'm forever grateful that I sought mental health treatment and landed one of the best counselors, who partnered with and helped to save me.

I'm Eric Jones, Jr., a medically retired army veteran, who served from 2012 to 2020, including three tours overseas. This is my story and I hope it will help anyone that reads this, who may be going through a mental health struggle, to seek help.

Get a counselor. It's never too late.

Much love and stay blessed.
Eric Jones, Jr.

ABOUT ERIC JONES, JR

ERIC JONES JR is a retired US Army veteran and the host of The Eric The Great Podcast which brings the best musicians, artists, entertainers, and high-profile business minds under one banner where Mental health awareness, treatment, and resources are frequently discussed. He is a mental health advocate and has recently added actor to his bio, with a featured role in *Dance For Me*, a BET original movie.

Follow Eric on Social Media:
 Facebook: https://www.facebook.com/ERICJPODCAST
 Instagram: www.instagram.com/ericjthegreat
 Instabio: Instabio.cc/403290099GDK3

JULAINE

The path to purpose is often not the route you expect. Sometimes, the journey takes a different, broken course. The one thing you can be certain of is that God wastes nothing! Like Kintsugi, He mends all the broken pieces with the priceless gold of His love and uses it all to make something beautiful ... because you are worth it!

CHAPTER 2
PATH TO PURPOSE

"IN RETROSPECT"—SOMETIMES, that is the way you finally make sense of your life experiences. It's in retrospect that you see that everything happened for a reason and led you to purpose. It's in retrospect that the pieces come together ... because God works that way. That is my story. Now, I see it, but had I been asked three years ago, I certainly would not have seen the value in my past, my mistakes, and my pain. I would not have thought anything good could come of the mess that was my life. Or, so I felt. It's funny how hindsight can give a new perspective on the things you don't understand when you're in the middle.

I am the last of seven children. We were all raised in a Christian home and I knew all the 'right' things to do, so I did them. I just existed. No one could have told me in my formative years that my life had a purpose. I didn't see it. Actually, I didn't think about it. I knew the rules to follow, so I complied with little thought about who I was, what I wanted, or where my life would end up. I had no recognition of the fact that God had a purpose for me or my life, or that I needed to be deliberate about living.

We were not taught these things in the church. We were taught right and wrong. If you did right, you went to heaven. If you did wrong ... well ... you didn't. In church, you weren't taught how to identify your feelings or how to deal with them. You were told how you should feel. Any thoughts or feelings outside of the scripted ones were bad and you needed to be a better Christian, get prayed for ... or get delivered. I lived this way for most of my life—shut in by expectations.

My life followed the path of least resistance all the way up until I was thirty-eight years old. And even then, I wasn't sure what purpose my life served or what I wanted to accomplish. Up to that point, I knew what my life was supposed to look like, and so worked hard to ensure that it did.

I had life scripted. The perfect home, job, marriage, and family—or at least, so it seemed to everyone around me. No wonder so many were left in shock when I walked out of my marriage of over fifteen years. I left my marital home with two children and what could hold in my car. The façade I had created was done so well and for so long that even I believed it sometimes, but I couldn't any longer.

I was dying every day, slowly ... and I don't think anyone understood it but me. Only I understood how much I felt shut in and stuck. The pain became tangible. I felt it every day in every fiber of my being. I was shut in by my fears and insecurities that had plagued me through all my years, and— by that point—shut in because I had no confidence in the fact that God had a plan for my life, especially because of the mess I had made of it. I had no confidence that He still had a way to get me from where I was, to the destination He had prepared for me.

God has a way of taking your lowest moments and turning them into your biggest testimony. It was in the place of my greatest pain and brokenness that He met me. That place became the catalyst for who I have become. The process ... the journey ... was all but easy, and still isn't. It's different. I've had to learn about myself. I've had to identify toxic patterns and when I'm not being authentic. I've had to unlearn things that I've been taught all my life, and relearn things ... God's way. I can't tell you about all the tears I've cried in this process. But ... I'm stronger and happier. I know who I am in God and learning more each day. The lessons I've been taught and the value I have found in my pain and my past could only have come through the process. And it prepared me for my purpose.

The Process

I have known deep pain and deep regret. From the moment I got married, I knew I was living a lie. Our marriage was plagued with untruths and infidelity from the outset. Looking back, I realize we were both broken. Each of us had scars and trauma that we should have spent time to heal before ever walking down that aisle and saying 'I do'. But we didn't know. We took the plunge, then we got shut in by expectations, family, the church, our friends, our misguided ideals … shut in with no apparent way out.

So, we suffered in silence, thinking we had no choice. Only we knew that we were not okay. If I'm honest, we tried … we tried to be happy and make it work, but we were never honest with God, ourselves, or each other, and so couldn't truly heal. That is a hard place to be. The most overwhelming feeling for me during those years was unhappiness. Deep-rooted unhappiness that intensified with each passing year and, in the end, had me feeling like I'd rather not live than continue to exist that way.

In 2016, after eleven years of marriage and all the drama that came with it, I remember crying out to God in utter desperation for deliverance one way or the other. I prayed for healing in my marriage, and my heart. I prayed for understanding. I prayed for my husband, and for him to change. I even formed a prayer group and prayed with those ladies for thirty days for our husbands. I was desperate. What I have found is that God moves in our desperation. Often, we don't include Him until then.

Slowly, things began to change, but not in the way I expected. God told me from his word in Isaiah 54:11 that he would rebuild my foundation. That made me happy! "Thank you, Lord!" my heart sang. What I didn't realize at the time was that in order to 'rebuild' my foundation, it would first have to be destroyed … and so began the process.

Things grew progressively worse at home. There was such a breakdown and so much heartache, but we kept the picture of perfection for

FROM STUCK TO LIMITLESS   17

everyone to see. Eventually though, if you were observant, you would notice that we weren't doing well. I sought refuge in a friendship that ended up as an adulterous relationship. But it brought such comfort. I reasoned with God about it, telling myself I had every right, having lived through his unfaithfulness. I even began to believe this relationship was 'of God'... crazy, I know. But hurt and sin will make you crazy.

I now understand why the Bible teaches that sin brings death. I was dead inside. I showed up for everything—work, church, my family, the kids, all of it, but I was dead inside. This is why God desires to protect us from sin. He doesn't want us to live that way. This is why He creates boundaries and rules for us to abide by. What I have also learned, is that God's grace is sufficient.

Eventually, the situation became too much for us to continue, and in July 2020, I left my home and marriage. So began my testimony of "what the enemy meant for evil, God turned it around for my good." Though I didn't see it all then, today I see that God used everything! He didn't cause anything to happen. Those were my decisions ... but He used everything. That moment, when the world of fake perfection I built came crashing down, was the start of fulfilling my purpose and realizing God's promises. You couldn't have told me that then, but I see it now.

The Here and Now – The Purpose

Over the last three years, God has taken me on a journey of self-discovery and learning, that I would never have thought possible. The best years of my life are the present, and that started with a breaking. The lessons I have learned in my process of healing have allowed me to support others at work, in my family, and in my friendship circles in ways I would never have been able to, had I not experienced life the way I did. The pain was for a purpose; the path was for a reason.

My passion for teaching people to know, understand, and love themselves—especially before committing to another—was born out of all I have experienced. My life's purpose is to advocate for showing up authentically, especially in Christendom. I have a God-given vision to impact the lives of many with the truth that it's okay to show up as both blessed and broken. God doesn't mind. In fact, He wants you that way. Your brokenness does not discredit your purpose. Your experiences are firm ground for you to become an expert. Someone needs that! God won't waste that! But you must show up.

I have discovered my purpose. And it started when I showed up as my authentic, broken self. When I came to the end of me, I learned that God stood there, waiting, with the plan He had all along … and that nothing was wasted. Not one thing. The pain brought me here. The process taught me lessons. The path took me to purpose. You may *feel* shut in, but that is the time to lean into God. Let Him become your confidante. Show up in all your brokenness — just as you are — and let Him work on you, and in you, and eventually through you for His glory.

It may *feel* like you are shut in, by your pain, your mistakes, your past, your trauma, but you are not. You are in a cocoon. That is where you develop your wings, because you were meant to fly. Don't despise where you have been, or where you are. The words in Zechariah 4:10 ring true. "Do not despise these small beginnings, for the Lord rejoices to see the work begin" (Life Application Study Bible). You may not see it now, but I promise He will make all things beautiful in His time if you just trust Him. He has big plans for your small steps of obedience in faith.

In recent times, I discovered a quote by the late, great Maya Angelou that says, 'Do the best you can with what you know until you know better. Then when you know better, do better'. You can't do until you know, and you can't know until you've learned. Give yourself the grace to learn the lessons. Each person's path is different, but if we let it, our path always leads to the Saviour.

He waits with arms outstretched, wanting to make His promises true and help you live out your purpose and your best and happiest life. Let Him. Understand that your path to the best version of you will be anything but perfect, and even when you begin to walk toward Him, you will misstep.

Here's the thing, He knows that too, and He doesn't care … just keep walking. As you walk, you will make your way out of that place where you feel shut in, and you will realize that you were never buried, just planted. Now is your time to bloom and grow. You are not alone … and you are not shut in.

With all my love,
Jules on Purpose

ABOUT JULAINE ROBINSON

JULAINE IS a Christian and mother of two. She is the last of seven siblings, who grew up in rural Jamaica. She has had over twenty years of experience working in the financial sector.

Though her secondary and post-secondary education focused on business and finance, she moved from that industry in January 2023 to pursue her passion for counseling, life coaching, and managing mental health.

She holds an Associate Degree (First Class Honors) in Human Resource Management and is currently pursuing a BSc. in Guidance and Counselling. Her desire is to use her learning and experience to impact youth and young adults, so they learn to embrace themselves authentically, manage emotions responsibly, overcome challenges and mistakes, and discover the best version of themselves.

Julaine works as the Administrative Director at D'Marie Institute Limited, an institution that works to balance beauty and manage mental health. Through D'Marie, she supports clients in developing and managing life habits for good mental health through motivational speaking and Mental Health Workshops.

Follow Julaine on Social Media:
Instagram: https://bit.ly/JulesonInstagram
& Thoughts by Jules bit.ly/ThoughtsByJules
Facebook: https://bit.ly/JulesonFacebook

MINDI

Labels are a way of categorizing and grouping people based on certain traits or characteristics, perceived or real. These may be positive or negative, and can have a significant impact on the way we see ourselves and interact with others. Unfortunately, many people are "tagged" by others without their consent, and these classifications can be both limiting and harmful.

Negative labels can be particularly damaging, as they can create a self-fulfilling prophecy where the person internalizes the associated qualities and starts to believe that it defines them. For example, someone who is thought to be "lazy" may start to believe they are inherently laid-back and become unmotivated as a result.

It's important to recognize that the way we classify people is often based on biases or limited information, and may not reflect the complexity of a person's identity or experiences. While labels can be useful for categorization and understanding, it's important to be mindful of their limitations and avoid using them as a way of defining people or making assumptions about them.

One way to combat this negative impact is to focus on individual strengths and abilities. Rather than concentrating on a person's perceived or actual weaknesses or shortcomings, it's important and better to recognize and celebrate their unique talents and contributions. By cheering others on for their individual strengths and abilities, we can create a more inclusive and understanding society.

CHAPTER 3
"SAUCY"

JUNE *1998*

Mindi,

Congratulations on your graduation. You are saucy, creative, and comfortable to be with. May this period of sadness pass quickly and your gentle spirit shine brightly as you emerge into your adulthood.

This inscription was written inside a small book called The Law of Success by Paramahansa Yogananda. The kind wishes were the words of the director at the massage school where I had just graduated, and the palm-size book was her parting gift. It was a book of wisdom I could not yet comprehend. All I saw was the glaring word in black ink under my name; saucy. I was fixated. At only twenty-three years old, I had already been called that numerous times. I still did not know what it meant. But, my twenty-three-year-old self did not like it, and I intrinsically knew it implied something was profoundly different and wrong with me. Good girls were not saucy.

It is hard to decipher where my self-loathing started. Anyone who has lived through trauma and battled the demons of self-hatred and doubt will tell you that timelines, dates, and memories are not always fluid, sensible, or clear. Memories are tied to emotions, and they come in waves. However, there are vivid visions of the Nutcracker at a big, beautiful theatre in downtown Chicago during a magical winter, paired with the knowledge that the Plum Fairy was sweet, but I was not. The boy and girl traveling across the board playing Candy Land were well-behaved and nice. I was not. The children gathered for the kindergarten class photo flashed obligatory smiles as instructed. I did not.

In public, strangers stopped and told my mother I was adorable. She would correct them and say, "When's your birthday? You can have her as a gift. Then you'll see just how adorable she is." When I misbehaved, she often told me she would change my name to Sister Mary Magdalena and send me to live at a convent; I guess that is where my inner hatred began. I believed I was bad because I was told I was. Saucy just sounded like a more descriptive version of bad.

It's not hard to write the story of the "abused girl" who turns into easy prey. Pedophiles are skilled and cunning, and prepare for their hunt with great precision. A rambunctious little girl who often misbehaves and has a busy single mother is a ready-made target. She is like a wounded animal abandoned out in the Sahara; a perpetrator spots her from miles away. The story writes itself. It could not have been easier. I was already conditioned to believe I was bad.

Being around a grown man who told me I was good felt like salvation. It felt warm. It felt fun. It was the opposite of punishment and the opposite of bad. His attention felt like love. I was taught it was love. I wonder if the wounded animal lying helpless in the desert must, at first, just for a second—maybe with confusion—look at the oncoming hunter as if they may possibly be there as a savior. Right before the kill, there is a moment of peace and calm ... pleasure. I know.

I was seven. Turning eight. I couldn't memorize my multiplication tables. I was laughed at in class because I spelled the number after seven on the board as ate. I was dumb and slow, and of course, I was bad. I did not know then how desperately I was trying to survive. I had no mental bandwidth to memorize spelling words or understand what nine times seven totaled. My body was learning things faster than my mind, and there was no way to make sense of it. He said

FROM STUCK TO LIMITLESS 27

Mommy would be mad if I told. And only bad girls made their mommies angry. How could I allow myself to be worse?

At age sixteen, I learned how much worse I could be. I was the whore who ruined my mother's relationship. She told me so. I was selfish and stupid. But I did know how to get love, because sex was love. I was good at that and had perfected turning sex into my only asset. I thought I was the good kind of bad. I laughed in the face of the woman a few blocks away who forbade her precious and innocent daughter from being my friend. I was a "bad influence." She told me I was saucy. Secretly, that hurt me to my core and filled me with shame.

That same year, I was drugged and gang-raped. The group of derelicts left me naked and unconscious in an elevator. I woke with a familiar sense of shame that was under the surface all along. I did not report it and never discussed it with anyone other than my girlfriend, who was there, doing her best to intervene. There was no reason to discuss it. The attack was my fault and what I deserved. I believed I would be punished for what happened, and really, who would care anyway? I was just a dumb girl who always gave it away, regardless. The little self-respect I had dissipated. I became comfortable with my new identity—a dumb, saucy, bad girl.

When I was twenty-three, a man assaulted me right after I graduated from massage school and received The Law of Success. I thought he was a friend. I sobbed that entire night and replayed every word and every motion. What was wrong with me? Why was I so damaged and gross that I caused this to happen over and over? What did people see when they looked at me? Was it inevitable that I was always going to be the prey? I had no voice, power, or belief that I deserved better. I did not know an alternative. I was exhausted when the sun rose the following day, and my eyes were swollen. But I had made peace with the facts. This was my life. I was meant to be punished. I was destined to be the bad girl and carry all the baggage that came with the label. That morning, I truly believed that about myself.

What happened afterward was the turning point of my story and life. The days following my assault were filled with support, understanding, validation, and love. The man I love, his family, and my friends listened without judgment or blame. This was the real kind of love that I yearned for, that honored my past, and educated me about violence. I learned that nothing I did at age seven, sixteen, or even twenty-three caused people to hurt me. They were solely responsible for their actions.

I came to understand that there was no shame in the things that had happened to me. I did not choose them, and had no reason to believe the lies I had been fed. The people that are my family today lifted me and told me the real truth about myself; I am smart. I am brave. I am deserving of goodness. I am goodness. And most of all, I don't believe I am to blame.

It took time and still takes time, but I learned that I am more than my body. I learned that my body is powerful, healthy, muscular, and strong. I can do things with my body and for my body that are for my pleasure and no one else's. My body belongs to me, and it has completed bike races, 5Ks, hikes, fire walks, floatation tanks, sweat lodges, and sound baths. My body has had more experiences and sensations than I thought possible, all of my own choosing.

I learned sex and love are different, and both can be beautiful. I learned how to receive and give love fully. I learned that these are my rights and that violence and coercion play no role in this equation. I learned how to ask and how to trust. I learned to honor that I am still learning, and that fact is okay.

Today, I respect all my experiences and the journey that led me to the woman I am at this moment. It is sometimes a challenge to face the old emotions and memories where I feel small, weak, shameful, or stupid and insignificant, but I am reminded that I was victimized … but I am not a victim. I am more than that and more than just surviving. I am victorious. I can choose to allow myself to believe those old lies and give power to those words, or I can write a new belief for myself. I choose the latter.

I am honored today to work with survivors of rape and sexual abuse, both men and women, young and old, at the nonprofit I started a decade ago. Their stories remind me of the common theme of resiliency and strength we all share. I am grateful for every chance I get to be in the presence of a brave survivor finding their voice for the first time. That gift gives me hope.

As I approach fifty, I am a woman who embraces growth and the good fortune to continue learning. I am whole, passionate, vibrant, and wide open to possibilities. I don't have all my memories. I still don't like The Nutcracker or the game of Candy Land. My multiplication and spelling stink. I am perfectly imperfect and complex. I am unabashedly good. I am saucy.

Mindi Fetterman

ABOUT MINDI FETTERMAN

MINDI IS the Founder and Visionary Leader of The Inner Truth Project. She is a wife, a mother, and a career woman. She is also a survivor of physical and sexual abuse as a child, drug facilitated sexual assault, gang rape as a teenager, and assault as an adult.

Though by "conventional wisdom" Mindi Fetterman's story shouldn't read as it does, the hurdles and experiences she has faced have fostered an incredible commitment to community, activism, and leadership that is changing lives each and every day.

After struggling through her childhood and teenage years, Mindi began a path to sanity and sobriety in her twenties. She graduated from Florida Atlantic University, Magna Cum Laude, with a degree in Women's Studies. Her education fostered the activist within, and she spent five years counseling women and providing clinic defense at Presidential Women's Center in West Palm Beach, Florida. The experience helped her to develop a strong voice and passion for political and community activism, and today Mindi continues to stand up for reproductive and healthcare choices for women and their families.

In the past several years, she has traveled to Brazil to work in schools and orphanages, has volunteered for and been recognized by Hospice, Big Brothers Big Sisters, Sarah's Kitchen, Planned Parenthood, The Children's Healing Institute, The Eckerd Foundation, and numerous autism organizations.

She is a board member of the Florida Council Against Sexual Violence, a member of the National Coalition of Jewish Women, Hadassah, and The Port St. Lucie Business Women. Mindi has had the pleasure of serving on many boards that help local women, children, and families, including the St. Lucie County Education Foundation, Emergency Medical Association, St. Lucie County's Substance Abuse Coalition, The Treasure Coast Jewish Film Festival, Safe Space, and Pace Center for Girls.

Mindi is the Founder and Past Board President of the St. Lucie County Chapter of National Organization for Women, and former Membership Chair of the St. Lucie County League of Women Voters. She's the grateful recipient of the United Way of St. Lucie County 2012 Community Angel Award, Special Honor Award Winner from Palm Beach County NOW in 2013, the 2014 Soroptimist International Volunteer of The Year, and a recipient of the 2015 Jefferson Award. She received the Community Impact Award from The Children's Services Council of St. Lucie County in 2019, the Bob Graham Distinguished Service Award from Indian River State College in 2020, and The Visionary Voice Awards presented by the National Sexual Violence Resource Center in 2021.

For years, Mindi has been frequently invited as a guest speaker to different venues to candidly discuss her experiences with breaking the ties of shame that exist in society around sexual violence, rape, and incest. In so doing, she realized the severe shortage or outright absence of services on the Treasure Coast for survivors like herself.

Realizing a decade long dream of opening a center for survivors of sexual trauma, in December of 2012, Mindi founded the only secular nonprofit exclusively for survivors of sexual violence, The Inner Truth Project, and in the spring of 2013, opened the Inner Truth Center to provide loving support, encouragement, education, and healing for survivors and their families. The response has been overwhelming, enlightening, and most importantly, affirming that alone survivors may suffer—together, they can heal and thrive.

Born in Chicago, Illinois, Mindi has lived in Florida for over thirty years. She and her husband Adam were married in Asheville, N.C. in 1999 and have an amazing son, Noah. When she isn't working, you can find her with her family at music festivals, in her kayak or camping. She is also a avid reader and loves foreign films.

Follow Mindi on Social Media:
   https://innertruthproject.org/

MARVA

We are often told, "Never have regrets." But is that wise?

One of my deepest regrets is that no one taught me the importance of taking the best care of myself. What healthy eating should look like, the importance of sleep and rest, and that exercise is medicine. I had to learn the hard way, which almost cost my life.

It doesn't have to be that way for you. Today is your day to begin learning true self-love. Loving yourself enough to do all you can to be the healthiest version of yourself.

CHAPTER 4
NO HEALTH ... NO WEALTH

THE PHRASES "HEALTH IS WEALTH" and "No Health, No Wealth" are not just cliches. As Josh Billings stated, "Health is like money, we never have a true idea of its value until we lose it,"

Our health is not something we should take for granted but instead, be our top priority in life. What is the point in accumulating money and wealth, building a successful business and career, and being famous with the best family and friends, if we are not well enough, or around, to enjoy these things?

There is a severe Health and Wellness crisis around the world. Obesity and overweight are at an all-time high. According to the World Health Organization (WHO), worldwide obesity has nearly tripled since 1975. Rates of overweight and obesity continue to grow in adults and children.

These two afflictions are major risk factors for many chronic health issues and diseases, such as heart disease, stroke, diabetes, kidney disease, inflammatory conditions such as arthritis, and even some cancers.

I was thirty-eight years of age, overweight, sick, and feeling like I was going to die. Drugs were of no use. My cardiologist told me that without a heart transplant, I probably wouldn't live. My heart was weak and barely pumping. I felt tired, lightheaded, and lethargic all the time. Plagued with shortness of breath, I slept in a recliner in an upright position every night.

At the same time, I experienced anxiety, insomnia, palpitations, severe depression, and shortness of breath. I was also plagued with gastric reflux, H Pylori, irritable bowel syndrome, recurrent urinary tract infections, and crippling arthritis.

As if these were not enough, I developed severe allergies to foods, cosmetics, and the environment. Due to this condition, I lost over thirty pounds in just a few weeks.

A successful cardiac ablation was done.

"A cardiac ablation is a procedure that scars tissue in your heart to block irregular electrical signals. It is used to treat heart rhythm problems." (Mayo Clinic)

My cardiologists gave orders to:

- Exercise for thirty minutes every day
- Get rid of coffee and any caffeinated drinks
- Decrease my stress level
- Try Yoga
- Get eight hours of sleep at night
- Eat healthily and take care of myself

I was desperate to live, to feel good in my body, mind, and spirit, so I followed the doctor's orders. That was twenty-two years ago.

You, too, deserve to be healthy, strong, and vibrant at whatever stage you are in life. You deserve to wake up feeling alive and strong every morning. I am committed to inspiring, encouraging, motivating, and educating *you* to become and remain the healthiest and fittest version of yourself. To lose the excess body weight and keep it off for good, knowing that it is possible for you if you are willing to do the work.

The healthy lifestyle is *not* as complicated as you think.

Too many people are dying prematurely from heart disease, diabetes, cancer, and other lifestyle-related diseases. And, too many are disabled due to arthritis, dementia, kidney disease, obesity, strokes, and other preventable lifestyle diseases and conditions.

Children, young, middle-aged, and older adults alike are being affected by many of these conditions. It is time that we take back our health, take back our lives.

It is time to be sick and tired of being sick and tired. To make the decision that enough is enough. To decide to do something about *your wealth, your health.*

Eat to Live. Choose Healthy Foods

There is a common belief that eating healthy is too expensive. I want to reassure you that although this might be true, in general, there are some things you can do to offset the cost. Here are a few tips to help you eat healthily on a budget:

- Plan your meals.
- Make a shopping list and stick with it.
- Use coupons.
- Buy store/generic brands.
- Buy healthy items on sale. For example, oatmeal is sometimes on sale at my local grocery store. I stock up at that time.
- Prepare home-cooked meals.
- Buy fruits and vegetables when they are in season. Prices are usually cheaper.
- One-pot meals are great. Cook enough for a few days and reheat. Take some to work for lunch.
- Beans and peas are cheap protein foods and are super healthy. A great alternative to expensive food items.

I go to Walmart once per month and stock up on beans, peas, wild rice, quinoa, and other healthy non-perishables, saving a lot of money. Cook your meats with cabbage, carrots, and collard greens, which are usually cheaper veggies. Other strategies you can use:

- Buy produce that is slightly dented and is usually marked down
- Buy in bulk at establishments like Costco or other wholesale farmers markets
- Grow your own produce

Exercise is Medicine Without Negative Side Effects

I cannot emphasize enough the importance of combining healthy nutrition with regular moderate exercise for the best results. Thousands of years ago, Hippocrates stated that, "Walking is man's best medicine." Walking is beneficial in so many ways and it is free. Walking helps to:

- Maintain a healthy weight
- Improve your blood pressure
- Strengthen your muscles
- Energize your body
- Strengthen your bones
- Ensure you sleep better
- Reduce pain
- Improve your mood and spirit
- Improve your immune system
- Improve digestion
- Ensure we live longer and healthier lives

Find a walking buddy. Have set days and times to exercise. Decide on a venue in advance. If you skip an exercise day, make it up the next day, if possible.

Remember that you cannot exercise off a bad diet. It is imperative that you combine healthy eating with regular exercise to achieve your goal to get fit and stay fit, to get healthy and stay healthy, and attain and maintain your ideal weight. Start slow and build up. Baby steps lead to bigger steps.

Remember that health is long-term. It is a lifestyle. You are in this for the long haul and the benefits are worth your efforts. Healthspan is more important than lifespan. You want to be in excellent health for the duration of your life, whatever that period is ... free from severe or chronic diseases. This can be accomplished if you embrace a holistic health approach.

The Importance of Sleep

It is while you sleep that your body repairs and restores itself. Adequate sleep even helps with weight loss. Research has pointed to optimal sleep being seven to eight hours per night. Lack of sleep can lead to hypertension, rapid heart rate, increased inflammation, weight gain, and even affects your immune system. Adults should aim to get seven to eight hours of good quality sleep at night, children need more.

Hydrate Properly

Did you know that about 60% of your body is water? Many people walk around every day in a dehydrated state. Oftentimes, that lack of energy, the headache, that chronic constipation, the frequent urinary tract infection, that annoying muscle pain, is a result of dehydration.

Stay hydrated. Coffee is a diuretic and can lead to dehydration. If the weather is cold, drink warm herbal teas or warm water infused with fruits or veggies, like cucumber.

Enjoy your life

- Be sure to make time for rest, relaxation, and fun.
- Spend time in nature and get plenty of sunlight, our natural source of vitamin D.
- Find a reason to laugh
- Go out and meet new people
- Take yourself on a date
- Celebrate your wins, no matter how large or small
- Live in the moment
- Slow down and savor the beauty around you
- Listen to the birds, smell the roses

• • •

If you embrace these holistic health tips, you will be well on your way to being the healthiest and best version of yourself.

In just a few months, I will celebrate my sixty-first birthday. I wake up every day feeling strong and energetic, with no health issues. I have been at my ideal weight for many years. I'm happy and living my best life now. So can you.

Our past does not dictate our present or future state. If you are willing, you, like me can make a few simple lifestyle choices to reverse those health challenges that you are dealing with, or prevent any issues that may be lurking around the corner. It is never too late to begin. Start slow and build up.

Several years ago, during my physical, emotional, and spiritual health crisis, I discovered the power of prayer, meditation, and mindfulness. In my search, I understood that the answers I sought were inside me. I learned to look within wherein lies my peace, joy, contentment, and happiness. Since we are whole beings, health must therefore be addressed from a holistic standpoint: Body, Mind, and Spirit.

You can only be successful in attaining health and well-being when you embrace the philosophy of holistic health, understanding that the whole person is made up of interdependent parts, and if one area isn't working properly, then all other parts will be negatively affected.

Discipline and self-control are necessary to succeed. These are learned through daily practice. Practice leads to progress.

I live what I teach and it works.

Marva Riley

ABOUT MARVA RILEY

MARVA RILEY IS A REGISTERED NURSE, who advocates for a Holistic Lifestyle, which includes eating well, with a diet rich in vegetables, fruits, legumes, nuts, grains, roots, and minimizing meat and flesh.

A native of the island of Jamaica in the West Indies, she immigrated to the US in 1989 with her two children and husband.

In her late thirties, Marva was diagnosed with a life-threatening heart disease, severe depression and insomnia, bowel diseases, crippling arthritis, and severe food and environment allergies. These debilitating conditions forced her to adopt a healthier way of living. After much research and the testimonials of thousands of people, Marva ate her way to her healing with a plant-based diet

Fast forward a few years, Marva now enjoys a vibrant and healthy life. She has learned how to be creative in her kitchen as she adds her favorite healthy seasonings and spices to whip up the most delicious foods.

She is the author of three health and wellness books: *Eat Sleep Meditate A Nurse's Guide to Health, SHEIR Recipe book (Simple Healthy Easy Inexpensive Recipes)*, and her most recent publication, *Lose Weight & Keep it Off for Good Understanding the Weight Loss Game.*

Her passion is to encourage, inspire, motivate & educate so that everyone can become and remain the healthiest version of themselves.

Follow Marva on Social Media:
Facebook: https://www.facebook.com/marva.riley.73
Instagram: https://instagram.com/marva.riley.73
YouTube: https://youtube.com/@marvariley

BRIDGETT

My Path to Freedom: For decades, I believed my looks were all that I had to offer in relationships and I spent a lot of time focusing on my appearance, knowing that was how I'd attract a mate. However, the inner me was a complete mess and my dysfunctional ways were mostly the cause of subsequent breakups. Then I made the decision to practice celibacy so I could focus on myself as a whole. It was time well spent.

CHAPTER 5
I'VE BEEN CALLED WORSE

THEY TELL you never look your best when going to the Veterans Affairs Hospital after applying for disability. It's supposed to give the impression that you're either financially broke, or spiritually broken to the extent of avoiding personal hygiene. The ill-advised always took heed. My saggy, faded jeans and grey sweatshirt was the perfect attire. I completed the look with one of my less-appealing wigs and just a hint of makeup.

Being almost unrecognizable, I sat patiently in the waiting room rehearsing what I would, and would not, disclose about my personal flaws. Then a half-hour later, a VA psychiatrist called me into his office.

The layout was nothing like I'd anticipated. No educational credentials proudly displayed. No framed inspirational quotes strategically placed throughout. Not even a comfortable couch to lounge across if I decided to spill my guts. You'd think any caring psychiatrist would go out of his way to design his office to be more conducive to the abnormal mind. But not this one. Dr. Compassionate apparently didn't deem it necessary.

He extended one hand, gesturing for me to have a seat in a cheap aluminum chair. Though I obliged, I continued scanning his office making mental notes of all the abnormalities only the self-absorbed would miss. Not a good first impression. Then I sat face to face with

Dr. Compassionate—the man the VA said I could trust with my most valuable asset ... my sanity.

The moment took me back to the principal's office in high school. My guess was the rules of engagement hadn't changed since then. Meaning that you never give away information for free, until you find out what the opposition discovers about you first. I crossed my legs and folded my hands neatly in my lap, like a well-bred debutante.

As I settled in, the room became still. I was paralyzed with anxiety. And just when I was about to lose the cat-and-mouse game we had going, he leaned into his wingback chair and asked in a rather soothing tone, "So, what brings you here?"

Fair question, but I wasn't about to let him off that easy—we'd met only moments ago. I'd been let down enough times trusting black men with my innermost thoughts. It was part of the betrayal that spiraled my life out of control. I'd be damned if I was going to give in so rapidly to an over-analytical white boy, though his deep, dark eyes radiated with sympathy and trust as they pierced through mine.

Nonetheless, I searched my brain for ways to articulate an answer that would prevent me from going too deep. Unfortunately, I couldn't remember a darn thing I'd rehearsed earlier. Instead, I turned away and focused on his bookcase.

Four shelves were crammed with textbooks, binders, and pamphlets. None of them aligned, based on height the way a normal person would arrange their bookcase ... just randomly placed on the shelves. Twelve on the first row, sixteen on the second, nine on the third, and another twelve on the bottom row.

One title captured my attention, Cognitive Processing Therapy for PTSD: A Comprehensive Manual. Anxiety had reached its peak. My inner six year old who wasn't allowed to go outside and play, emerged. Unprovoked, I cried. Not subtle tears, but heavy sobs accompanied by mucus oozing from my nose. I covered my face in shame as a poised Dr. Compassionate handed me a box of tissue.

Once I calmed myself, I realized there was no longer any point in trying to come off as having everything together. Besides, he already had access to my entire military medical records, and likely had me pegged the moment I crossed his threshold.

It was time for closure, so I laid it out straight, no chaser. Only instead of feeling defeated, I was at peace. The weight of the world had unchained itself from my soul. Then he posed another question that had me puzzled at first, "Let me ask you this, do you count random items, or do you type most verbal conversations on an imaginary keyboard?"

The answer was obvious, until I took a moment and realized my actions weren't normal. I leaned forward, tightly grasped the arms of my chair, looked him in the eyes, and whispered with the intensity of an F.B.I. interrogator. "I do both ... but how did you know that?"

"Because that's what individuals with chronic PTSD do. It's a way of keeping the mind occupied to avoid being triggered." He must've sensed I needed more reassurance, "... and it's a coping mechanism that's perfectly normal."

Finally, it all made sense. After twenty years of beating myself up over my alcohol abuse, dysfunctional relationships, along with tons of other suspect behavior, I was simply exhibiting the symptoms of PTSD. Then he either tested, or teased me, with a follow up question. "What have you counted since entering my office?"

The answer came strictly from memory. "The number of shelves—four. The number of books on each shelf—twelve, sixteen, nine, and twelve. The number of screws in the door—eighteen. The number of windowpanes—nine."

I could've gone on, but I rejoiced instead. This whole time my conflicting behavior was rational, because the symptoms of PTSD are normal reactions to abnormal events in life.

We talked openly for another twenty minutes. Of course, I couldn't leave without disclosing the horrid event I experienced on December 12, 2001 that happened in the Middle East, shortly after 9-11. I was convinced escorting dead bodies onto base was the catalyst that launched my descent into dementia.

After relaxing a bit more and feeling protected in his care, I wondered if his "disorderly" office was created by design—a means of naturally luring out evidence of an affliction. Dr. Compassionate indeed.

With my recovery now within arm's reach, we went over treatment plans. Afterward, it hit me how hard I unjustly viewed the Vietnam-era Veterans based on how they coped with PTSD. Until then, I'd never showed them the empathy they deserved. In fact, I downright called them out as faking mental disorders to avoid being productive members of society. Forgiving myself for those unsubstantiated conclusions became a part of my therapy as well.

Hallelujah! Even though I did it kicking and screaming, I finally triumphed in breaking the generational cycle of not seeking help in the form of psychological therapy. It is now a significant part of my self-care. Since reaching out to the VA for support, my quality of life has improved tenfold. I regularly hike, write, travel, perform community service, enjoy time with family and friends, and even started my business.

More importantly, I began the process of becoming a Certified Peer Specialist (CPS) through the Georgia Mental Health Consumer Network. A CPS provides peer support, working from the perspective of our lived experiences, to help build environments conducive to recovery. We promote hope, personal responsibility, empowerment, education, and self-determination in the communities we serve. Through our stories of triumph, our peers can recognize their recovery potential.

My journey has been amazing because being a CPS is a win-win. Not only do I get to help my fellow veterans, who are struggling with addictions and mental illnesses discover unique ways of living their best lives, my vocation also allows me to grow because I'm using the training and my own expertise to continuously empower myself.

Coming to terms with being a disabled Veteran has its challenges. I guess I can take comfort in the fact that people can't tell by looking at me—no visible scars, or missing limbs, only a socially impaired mentality. Also, I was blessed with the choice of seeking treatment for what ailed me. A lot of my comrades weren't as fortunate … taking their very last breaths on the battlefield, or in a makeshift hospital on foreign soil.

PTSD affects approximately three and a half percent of U.S. adults every year. Knowing that I'm not alone means everything. And if I learned to live and thrive with PTSD, I can survive anything.

Little did I know COVID-19 was right around the corner. Fortunately, I went into it armed with some powerful coping mechanisms, such as daily exercises, smarter food choices, and removing toxic people from my life. Those strategies worked well, along with what I consider the most instrumental benefit—that of having a network of individuals who teach, guide, and support me on all levels.

Bridgett Renay

ABOUT BRIDGETT RENAY

BRIDGETT RENAY HAS AUTHORED five best-selling titles on everything from fictional corporate drama to non-fictional business development. However, living life as an entrepreneur continues to be her real passion.

She is the President and CEO of Legacy Bridge, Inc., where the objective is to serve the undervalued and underserved individual into discovering their full potential through personal and professional development. This is achieved through self-help literature, online workshops, in-person lunch and learns, as well as motivational speaking.

Bridgett Renay began her professional speaking career, landing on the same platform alongside powerhouse speakers such as Lisa Nichols, Shellie Hunt, Robin Roberts, and Johnny Wimbrey ... to name a few. She also collaborates with individuals, non-profits, small businesses, civic organizations, as well as Fortune 500s.

She believes through utilizing leadership, time management, team-building, emotional intelligence, communication, conflict-resolution, along with other invaluable attributes, any individual can live their best life emotionally, spiritually, physically, socially, and financially, regardless of their upbringing or current environment.

While earning a Certificate in Women's Entrepreneurship from Cornell University, a Bachelor of Science in Technical Communication, and a Master of Business Administration, Bridgett Renay committed herself to excellence in all that she does.

The time spent growing professionally with 25-plus years in corporate America, and as a Retired Navy Reservist, tells the story of a journey that took her to faraway places, introduced her to intoxicating people, and shaped the way she views the world and her place in it.

Bridgett Renay resides in Riverdale, Georgia. When she is not running her business, or serving her community, she enjoys time with family and friends traveling to the world's most exotic locations as well as hiking scenic state and national parks with her hiking club, Team Train Faithfully.

Follow Bridgett on Social Media:
Facebook: https://www.facebook.com/bridgett.renay.3
Instagram: http://instagram.com/legacy.bridge
Twitter: https://twitter.com/BridgettRenay
Website: https://www.bridgettrenay.com
Free Download: https://www.bridgettrenay.com
Courses: https://lunch-break-hustlers.teachable.com/
PayPal Email: BridgettRenay@bellsouth.net

SOLSIRÉ

What do you do when you find yourself at a crossroad? Do you continue going down the path you're on, knowing it will set your future in stone, or do you seek God's mercy and try to build your life as best you can? Journey with me as I share my story of how, with God's help, I turned my life in a new and rewarding direction.

CHAPTER 6
GROWING UP BROKEN

The Lord is close to the brokenhearted and saves those
who are crushed in spirit.
Psalm 34:18 (New International Version)

THERE'S A SAYING THAT GOES, "A lot of fathers broke their daughter's heart long before any man," and, unfortunately, that was the case with me. So, while most dads I knew were their daughter's first love, my father was the scary monster I checked for underneath the bed.

Growing up broken, I always thought there was something wrong with me. That, somehow, I wanted the abuse to happen. How could I not, when I cried myself to sleep almost nightly, instead of telling my mother what was happening to her daughter, behind her and my brothers' backs?

I would like to share with you some of my most painful memories from being sexually abused, and what I did to overcome my suicidal thoughts.

One day, when I was seven years old, my mom went to check on my grandma, who was a heart patient. Mama, as we used to call her, lived fifteen minutes away from us so my mother usually cared for her. In the Netherlands, primary school children get their lunch break from twelve until one p.m. and, those who lived nearby had the luxury of going home during the day to enjoy a meal with their family.

We lived across the street from the school, and my mom always picked us up. So, you can imagine my surprise when one day I noticed my father standing at the gate instead of my mother. Grabbing my little brother's hand, I guided him toward the exit with my heart beating heavily in my throat.

Back then I didn't know what it was called yet, but apparently, I was having a panic attack.

Gino, who was about four years old at the time, held me close. "Why are you crying, Solsi?"

The little guy had no clue, and I wanted to keep it that way. It was my job as his big sister to protect him from the monster we called Dad. I would have given my all to keep him innocent.

"Nothing," I lied, drying my tears. "It's windy, my eyes always tear up when that happens."

He looked at me innocently with his big doe-eyes and dropped the matter.

My father grabbed our hands, scowled, and walked us home. He didn't like it when my mother went anywhere. From what I could tell, he'd just woken up and was in a bad mood. He usually didn't get up until the afternoon, as he would stay out late drinking and doing drugs.

At home, he fixed us something to eat and told my little brother to go sit in front of the television. "Your sister has been playing in the sandbox and has sand in her hair." He put on one of Gino's favorite shows, upped the volume, and dragged me to the bathroom with him.

Mind you, I hadn't played in the sandbox that day, which was why I already knew what was coming. Grabbing my flimsy shirt with shaking fingers, I unbuttoned and removed it in tears.

"Stop that," he ordered. "You know I love you, right?" Brushing his finger along my cheek, he added, "You're daddy's little girl, and mine alone." Yanking me by the arm, he pulled me into him. "If you ever let anyone other than me touch you, I will punish you severely."

I'll spare you the gory details, but let's just say I went back to school wishing I was dead. Not that anyone at school would've noticed because I had become somewhat of an expert at hiding my true feelings. I always managed to put a smile on my face in front of other people.

I went about my business and focused on my school work, which was the only silver lining that day. Until now, I can't recall what the subject was called, so I'm going to call it literary hour. Luckily for me, it was the first class. There, I devoured a book in one sitting.

Getting lost in a fantasy world was the only thing that kept me sane, until I began jotting down my suppressed feelings in a secret diary, which later evolved into poetry and short stories by the time I was eleven. I had become so good at putting my thoughts on paper that I found joy in creating poems and love letters for my classmates in high school. One of the poems I'm most proud of is the one I wrote for my cousin to propose to his girlfriend.

As I grew older, I started celebrating the small victories that shaped me into the woman I have become today—beginning with the incredible fact that my father had not managed to steal my sense of empathy, like he did with my innocence. Realizing from a young age that I was a good listener, I transitioned into a mother figure in high school. My friends always said that although I was their age, I had an old soul. Which I loved, by the way, because it was true.

At school, I spent hours mending my girlfriends' broken hearts, reminding them that life wasn't as black and white as it seemed, and that the heartbreak of a broken friendship or romantic relationship would eventually be less painful. Something I had to remind myself about on my off days, which happened more often once I hit puberty and the suicidal thoughts manifested.

Yet, as broken as I was back then, my people were my only kryptonite. Be it family or friends, I always wanted to make sure everyone was good and happy. Seeing as I couldn't be.

It might have been silly of me, but I even tried to understand my father's way of life so I could forgive him and finally remove the weight I had been carrying around. This came about when I started reading the Bible, and learned that forgiving someone wasn't for them but for your own soul and peace of mind. Thus began my quest to forgive, as forgiveness didn't mean to forget—something I still can't do.

It wasn't until I started that journey that I realized how sick he truly was. You see, according to a close family friend of his, my father had developed an alcohol and drug problem from an early age, due to being sexually abused as a little child. A secret he'd kept for my dad until he found out what my father was doing behind closed doors.

Instead of getting help to fight the demons living rent-free in his head, and breaking generational curses, he used me as his outlet. One of his all-time favorite lines was, "You're the only one who can make me feel better."

Finding out what he'd been through made me want to hurt him more than he'd already been hurt. Why should I have felt any kind of empathy for the man who'd been through hell and did the same to his daughter?

By the time I found out his history, he wasn't living with us anymore. A few years prior, when my mother discovered what he'd been doing to me, she called two of her brothers to remove him from our home immediately. He got more than he bargained for that day. I'm sad to say that I relished every minute of it, because to me it felt like redemption.

It was over for him the day I found the strength to break out of the cycle of abuse. I told my cousin, who told her mom. My auntie called my grandma, and she called my mother.

While my mom and her brothers kicked him out the same day, that didn't keep him from coming over at times to "check" on his kids— something he barely did when he was living with us because he didn't help my mother with anything. She was our mom and dad, and dare I say his mother, too? Instead of being a man, he was a little child who my mom clothed and fed daily. She also did her best to shelter me from him when he came to visit.

Back then, there was a real stigma surrounding sexual abuse.

Seeking therapy was not done in the 80s and 90s. Everything stayed covered up, as my family never shared their business with outsiders.

In my teens I spent most of my free time at my grandma's house, often sleeping there during the week. The times I spent at my "sanctuary", as I used to call it, were the best. I made some friends and played outside to keep my mind busy until it was nighttime and the bad dreams began.

Not knowing how to deal with my emotions, I grew more depressed and tried to take my life with pills. I still don't know how I got so lucky. But for God's grace, I'm still here.

When my first suicide attempt didn't work, I became bitter and often engaged in fights in school. I fought so much at that time because I was trying to feel anything other than the pain in my unsettled heart. Don't get me wrong, I was not a bully, but I never backed down from a fight.

I attended a coed school, so sometimes I even fought boys. I remember this one time when I hit a guy so hard, he fell to the floor unconscious, after he gave me a black eye. Another incident that scared me straight was when I smashed a guy's head through the window of a shop. He'd been bugging me and I didn't like people in my space. It's something that bothers me from time to time, and that's why I don't let just anyone touch me.

After that run-in, my oldest brother gave me two options. Either I went boxing with him to get my anger issues under control, or started going to church and Bible study with him. I choose the latter and have to admit it was the best choice. I felt like a child coming home to her father, my heart felt lighter, and the lump I carried around 24/7 in my throat slowly began to dissipate. Not only that, but I was more approachable as I began dressing like a girl instead of a boy.

While growing up, I didn't like wearing dresses because my body had filled out at an early age. I always tried to ignore stares from boys and men, who thought I was older than I really was.

For a moment there, I wanted nothing more than to become a nun, after seeing the musical *The Sound of Music* for the hundredth time with my grandma. Everything was going great. I even went and got myself a boyfriend, something I said I would never do—date. He was a cute Indian boy, who treated me right. Our relationship didn't last, because quite frankly, at that stage in my life I was still struggling with my deep-seated hatred toward men.

Alas, my joy was short-lived when I was remembered that I couldn't run from my past, as it would always catch up with me in the form of my father. The man just couldn't let me live my life in peace. I believe he wanted to see me as miserable as he was, something I fought daily not to become. Despite that, I was a heavy drinker in high school until I stopped myself.

————

There's another memory that to this day still hurts me more than words could ever describe ... We were at a club and a few of my brother's friends were fighting. My brother tried to intervene and stop the fight, only to get stabbed by accident. They rushed him to the hospital with a punctured lung and he stayed in there for a long-time, in recovery.

Instead of being by his son's side, like my mother was, my father came to our home and offered me money to sleep with him. "Don't act so innocent," he said. "I've been hearing you're a slut. I'm sure I'm not the only one who's offered you money for a little something."

I was home alone, and to say that I wanted to curl up and die would be an understatement. Luckily, my oldest brother got home a few minutes later and asked him to leave the house.

I dated a few boys after this nasty ordeal, but ended up wanting to hurt them because of my dad. Looking back, I regret judging them on my father's merits. Or, lack of them. Luckily, I'm somewhat at peace with my past behavior. I managed to stay friends with some of the guys who remained in my life even after our break up.

A few years later, I fell in love for real and began building a life for myself with my husband, whom I began dating in high school when I was fifteen years old. We stayed together through our junior and sophomore years and kept on dating in college until we became pregnant at the age of seventeen and moved in together after our son was born.

The day my oldest son, Djordano, was born was one of the happiest in my life. A few years later our joy multiplied, when we were blessed with our middle son, Joël. Six years after his birth, my third blessing, Jeremiah, was born.

My three sons became my heart, they meant everything to me. Loving my boys and being loved back by them unconditionally patched the holes in my heart. Their arrival erased all the memories of sexual abuse and the pain it had instilled in me.

I somehow managed to block everything from my mind until the day I came home and found my mother's lifeless body on the floor.

My poor mom died from a heart attack in her sleep and had rolled off the bed onto the floor. The trauma of her early demise set all my forgotten memories in motion as I cursed God, asking him why he'd taken my sweet mom instead of my evil father.

He died a year later from lung cancer. I remember hearing from my brother in Curaçao about him wanting to speak to me on his deathbed. To be honest, I didn't want to hear any of it, and cursed everyone out who so much as hinted that I should do the right thing.

In the end, after praying on it for days, I granted my father his last wish and forgave him for giving me such a bad start in life. In a strange way, I have him to thank for making me the strong woman I am today. I fought the beast and came out victorious in Jesus' name.

Luckily, I have not grown into the bitter woman I was so scared I'd become. My pesky demons still reside in my head and emerge from time to time, but something I will never do is give up. I owe it to my children to live.

Guess what? I finally started going to therapy after I wrote a series that didn't demonize my father, but instead redeemed him, giving him and my mother the happily-ever-after every child wants for their parents. He had found God as well in the last stages of his life.

At first it was hard talking about my issues, as it was instilled in our family that we didn't talk to strangers about important matters. Needless to say, it's been a long and hard road. But in my thirties, I finally understood that my father's actions didn't make or break me as I am not a victim but a survivor. One who wears her scars loudly and proudly. I've surrounded myself with a group of people who love and support me. Most of all, I've learned to love myself. All of me.

And now I dedicate myself to assisting others to straighten their crowns, reminding them that there are better days to come. Helping others who are stuck in a cycle of abuse—be it sexual, emotional, or psychological—is something I will never stop doing. They deserve to be free. Just as I am.

Solsiré E. Felida

ABOUT SOLSIRÉ E. FELIDA

SOLSIRÉ, a native of Willemstad, Curaçao, writes contemporary and romantic suspense, as well as paranormal romance.

Her current work is *Queen of Curaçao, Joey's Girl*, and *Ongelofelijke Dromen*. Her next project—*Love, Music & Everything in Between*—is set to release late in 2023.

When Felida isn't curled up with a good book and a tall glass of wine, you can find her in the kitchen as she loves to cook, bake, and everything else that has to do with food, including planning and catering events for family and friends for special occasions. She intends to release a cookbook someday soon.

For more info, please visit www.solsirefelida.com

Follow Solsire on Social Media:

Sociatap – https://sociatap.com/SeFelida

PATTY

No pastor wants to receive a 911 call about a church break-in. This incident created a horrible experience for Pastor Patty Harris as she was held hostage at gunpoint on the sidewalk of the church by two police officers who refused to believe a 'Black female' was the pastor of a predominately White congregation.

Accusing this well respected and beloved clergywoman of being the perpetrator, and treating her accordingly, was a light thing compared to the almost insurmountable amount of pain that plagued and nearly crippled her life and ministry afterward.

CHAPTER 7
POST TRAUMATIC GROWTH

IT WAS a call no pastor wants to receive while on the way to a board meeting. "Pastor, don't go in the Church. The silent alarm has gone off, there's an intruder. The police have been alerted and they are on their way."

I was in the parking lot when ten police officers arrived with the K-9 unit. The members of the K-9 unit sniffed me, sat, and crossed their paws as if to say, "It's Pastor Patty. She's okay."

An officer said, "Pastor, we'll go in and look around. We don't know if the intruder has a weapon, so you stand way over there on the sidewalk so you can be safe. Do you know how the intruder got in?"

"No, but here are my keys to the church. Try not to knock my doors down. New doors are not in the budget."

The officers laughed. "Pastor, you stand over there like we asked. We don't know what we'll encounter when we enter the church."

Several minutes later as I stood on the sidewalk, I heard something behind me and turned to see what it was. Two police officers stood with their weapons drawn. The officer closest to me had his gun trained on right temple. "Put your hands up now!" he yelled. "Who are you and what are you doing here?"

The other officer stood by the police car. The light on his gun was aimed at my chest. While slowly raising my hands, I explained, "I'm

FROM STUCK TO LIMITLESS 65

Pastor Patty, Officer. I'm the pastor of this church. Your colleagues are in there searching for a perpetrator. There was a 911 call."

"I know there was a call," he retorted. He looked at me with much disdain and unbelief. "You're the Pastor here at this church in this neighborhood? Why are you standing out here? I need to see some ID."

He questioned me as if an African-American female couldn't pastor a church in a predominantly white, suburban neighborhood.

"My wallet is in my pocket, sir."

"Get it!" he snapped.

I slowly reached into the pocket of my sweatsuit.

"I said, put your hands up," he shouted as he moved his weapon nearer to my temple and stood closer to me. Usually, at this time of day people were outside walking their child or dog. Why is no one out walking tonight, I thought.

"Why are you out here?" he shouted again.

Because his face was so close to mine, I looked in his eyes. I saw and sensed anger. It couldn't be from me. Something in his eyes oozed hatred.

I tried not to focus on the gun that he had now moved to my forehead.

"I need to see some ID."

The other officer was poised for action, yet he also seemed scared.

"Officer, my wallet is in my pocket. You can get it if you'd like."

Having sat in meetings with Chiefs of Police from across the state, and working with the local police department, I knew this officer was not following protocol. "I'm not getting it."

"I said, keep your hands up," he yelled.

"Officer, your colleagues are inside the church. You can call them."

"I don't have to call them. I want to know why you are standing out here."

"The officers told me to stand over here, away from the church because they didn't know what they would encounter inside."

He seemed to be getting more angry, and I was growing frustrated. "Well, Officer," I said, "you call Bud, your boss the Chief of Police and explain to him why you have your weapon pointed at Pastor Patty's head and holding her hostage at gunpoint."

Bud was the Chief's nickname. This officer looked at me as if I wasn't supposed to know that. He took a step backward, still holding the gun at my forehead. He looked at the other officer, who acted surprised as he hunched his shoulders. The officer with the gun to my forehead got on his walkie-talkie to call the officers inside the church.

He spoke into his walkie-talkie. "I have a Black female outside and she says she is the pastor of this church."

I frowned because this officer was also black. In fact, he was one of two Black officers in the entire police department.

The officer responded, "Does she have on a blue sweatsuit?"

"Affirmative," the officer said.

"Does she have glasses on and has curly hair?"

"Affirmative," he again responded.

"That is Pastor Patty. She is the pastor here."

The officer turned his walkie-talkie off, met the other officer's gaze and said, "Seems like she is the pastor here." He put his weapon in the holster and turned to walk away. "We can't be too careful. An officer was attacked in Philadelphia recently, so we're on high alert."

Both men got in the car and left me standing where they had found me. I walked a half block to a friend's house on the corner. Her husband was my assistant pastor. He wasn't home, so I shared my experience with her and she prayed with me. I told her I was okay and had to get back to the church. The other officers and the K-9 unit were still there.

I was on my porch across the street from the church when the officers exited the church. They met with me there and reported that they searched high and low and couldn't find anyone. Neither could they find a point of entry. They were kind and concerned, however, for some reason, I was afraid to tell them about the officers holding me at gunpoint.

After the officers left, I called a few friends and colleagues to share what had happened. Later that night after I fixed a mug of coffee and was ready to relax, something strange happened.

Little did I know, my life was about to turn upside down. As I sat to enjoy my mug of coffee, my hands shook uncontrollably. Coffee spilled everywhere. I couldn't catch my breath. My knees became weak. It felt as though something was rumbling inside me from my toes all the way up into my stomach. Was I having a heart attack? *Am I dying? What's going on? Lord Jesus, have mercy! My coffee is all over the floor.*

While trying to put the mug on the table, I cried uncontrollably.

Reflecting on the events earlier in the evening, I asked the Lord what that was about.

That incident marked the beginning of panic attacks and anxiety attacks, An overwhelming fear I had never known before, gripped me and would not let go. How could this be happening to me? Sleep left me. Every time I closed my eyes, I woke up sweating and in panic because all I could see was a gun in my face. I called my assistant and had him minister on Sundays and facilitate Bible studies.

It got worse before it got better. I became terrified of everything and everyone. Afraid to go outside, I didn't leave the house for weeks. I couldn't put a sentence together. This pattern lasted several weeks.

I had a prayer closet in my room. The only items in there were a Bible, notebook, pen, and a pillow. That had always been my secret closet where I communed with God, often for hours at a time. This was now where I lived. This was the only place I felt safe. I sat in my prayer closet for hours. During this time, I cried bitterly until I was exhausted. I prayed, no, I begged God to give me my mind back. I felt as if I had lost my sanity. I read the Bible, but couldn't comprehend what I was reading. I couldn't form an intelligent sentence. I began stuttering.

After about a month, I called a psychiatrist that I had worked with for a short time. She listened to my story. It took me awhile to get through it. Immediately, she wanted to put me on four different antipsychotic medicines. After I refused them, she cussed at me. I hung up on her.

Weeks later she called me, insisting that I take those medications. I was suffering from Post-Traumatic Stress Disorder. "You need these meds. You won't get through this without them. You're talking about people are praying for you, and your faith will get you through this." She cussed at me some more.

I told her to lose my number. I did not want to take those meds.

Each of them would cause too many adverse side effects. This was my choice.

With Post-Traumatic Stress Disorder, your mind continually rehashes a terrifying event as if it were in real time. Flashbacks of the event can occur at any moment. I constantly told myself, "You're safe now, Patty. You're safe. God is with you."

One night while crying in my secret closet, I heard a voice that simply said, "Write My Word."

I began to write the Bible, starting with Psalms. I couldn't understand anything I read or wrote.

Day and night, I continued to do this. Slowly, the fear lessened. I began to emerge and desire to engage with life. Not too much though. I had stopped driving, for fear I would have an anxiety attack, lose control of the car, and hurt someone. Although afraid, I walked to the bus stop to take a bus to the grocery store. Upon seeing a police car, I had an anxiety attack, and ran home screaming. So embarrassing for a pastor!

Months after I started getting better, being able to understand what I read, and able to talk, I still stayed in the house where I was comfortable and safe. No one came in, and I didn't go out. I grew comfortable with friends dropping food off for me on the porch. One day while in prayer, I had a revelation.

The officers held me hostage at gunpoint. Now I'm holding myself hostage. I have kidnapped myself. I won't go out, and I won't let anyone in.

I had to work harder for my freedom.

I had facilitated grief support groups at a Christian bookstore for many years. The manager, who texted me often, had told me she would drive me to the bookstore whenever I wanted to visit. She also reminded me they were praying for me daily.

I texted and asked her to pick me up the next day, and she did. The welcome was overwhelming. The staff gently embraced me. We cried together and stood in the front of the store as one big, hugging group. Thanking God for sparing my life, I returned to the bookstore for a couple days each week. This was another safe place for me. I was loved there. The panic attacks lessened. God was healing me through others, who had compassion for my battle for my mind.

I had resigned from pastoral ministry because I had to 'take care of me'. When I returned to pastoral ministry, it was almost a year later at a nursing home. I hadn't applied. I received a call asking if I would be the Director of Pastoral Care. The job was mine if I wanted it. I was still afraid to drive, so I took the bus and walked half a mile after getting to my stop.

What I encountered was more than one hundred seniors, many of whom had outlived their families. All they wanted from their pastor was love, someone to pray with, talk to, and share life with. I could do that. They, in turn, loved me unconditionally. I love my 'Senior Peeps'. God used them to further my healing and release me from my own self-kidnapping.

Fast forward to 2020. While at a pastors' conference, for the first time, I gave this testimony. Afterward, a lady came to me and gave me an officer's name. "He was the officer, wasn't he?"

I answered, "Yes, how did you know?"

She told me she knew in her heart he was the officer. "I believe he did want to shoot you. He hates Black women. He hates his mother."

She knew him, and said he was an angry man. "Pastor Patty, I'm so glad God spared your life. I have often prayed for him."

As she cried, we embraced and I prayed for this officer's salvation and healing through Jesus Christ.

Yes, PTSD is real. So is PTG.

Many people have never heard of Post Traumatic Growth. It is the personal growth that happens after a traumatic event. With PTG, people develop new personal strength, a greater appreciation for life, and even spiritual growth. Having been a hospital chaplain for thirty years and a crisis/trauma chaplain at Ground Zero in New York, I thought I was prepared for anything. Not! I wasn't ready for this event in my personal life. The only preparation I had was faith in God.

Our spirit, the part of us that communes with God, is never diseased. Although my mind couldn't understand what I read in the Bible, my spirit understood and was being fed by the Word. Whether I wrote it or read it, my spirit received it!

I have a new appreciation and pray for our Veterans, who return home from war coping with PTSD. I only had that one experience, which lasted about seven minutes. Many of our Veterans have lived this trauma daily. Keep them in prayer! Love and embrace them!

It takes much time, energy, and struggle to experience Post Traumatic Growth (PTG).

Psychiatrists call it PTG.

I call it Grace & Mercy!

Forgiveness was also a part of my healing. My mother always taught me that forgiveness is for me, not the other person. It sets me free from the root of bitterness, anger, and hatred, which will destroy my soul—if I let it.

He is still Jehovah-Rapha, the God Who Heals! Spirit, Soul, and Body

May you experience His divine healing in your life.

Pastor Patty Harris

ABOUT PASTOR PATTY HARRIS

PASTOR PATTY HARRIS has served in ministry for more than forty years. Having served as a pastor for twenty years, she has been a hospital and crisis/trauma chaplain for thirty years. She is the author of numerous books on Grief and Bereavement, Prayer, and Spiritual Formation.

A passionate psalmist, and teacher of the Word of God, conference facilitator, and revivalist, Pastor Patty also served as a crisis/trauma chaplain at Ground Zero in NY after the 9/11 terrorist attacks. She also served as an Associate Regional Pastor for American Baptist Churches of New Jersey. She has also served as a TV Producer and Engineer at TCT Christian Television.

She currently serves as Executive Director of Grief Relief Today Ministries, Inc. A ministry which serves the needs of grieving persons through books, media, in-person and online Grief Support Groups. She also serves as CEO of www.WJIL.Today, a 24/7 Gospel music/talk radio station where the mission is to educate, inform, and inspire people to reach their highest potential.

Pastor Patty's desire and passion is to help people to heal as well as grow in the grace and knowledge of the Lord Jesus Christ!

Follow Patty on Social Media:
    Website - http://www.WJIL.Today

BOOKS BY PASTOR PATTY:

Blessed Are They That Mourn

Comforting Those Who Grieve (Series)

Conquering Holiday Grief

Fear Nots for Everyday

Fear Nots For Those Who Grieve

God Has An APP For That

Praying in the Key of C (Series)

Restoring The Gates of Prayer

Surviving The Death of A Loved One

Thy Face Lord, Will I Seek

Follow Patty on Social Media:

Website - http://www.WJIL.Today

J.L.

"Hurt people, hurt people," is a popular phrase that describes the suffering and pain we see repeated in our world through individuals and relationships. People who have been traumatized in the past may unconsciously continue the same cycle.

By acknowledging their ordeal, we can better understand their reason for acting out. Through empathy, we can build trust, respect, and tolerance.

Also, the Creator has given us His Word as a guarantee that He can bring us out of any situation, no matter how challenging.

Isaiah 43:10-13 (New King James Version)

10 *"You are My witnesses," says the Lord,*
   "And My servant whom I have chosen,
   That you may know and believe Me,
   And understand that I am He.
   Before Me there was no God formed,
   Nor shall there be after Me.
   11 I, even I, am the Lord,
   And besides Me there is no savior.
   12 I have declared and saved,

I have proclaimed,
And there was no foreign god among you;
Therefore you are My witnesses,"
Says the Lord, "that I am God.
13 Indeed before the day was, I am He;
And there is no one who can deliver out of My hand;
I work, and who will reverse it?"

CHAPTER 8
HEALING THE HURT: BREAKING UNHEALTHY BEHAVIORAL PATTERNS

MEMORY LANE

Twenty-one years ago, two months after the birth of my son, I lost my mother. My sister is still alive, but I lost her before our mother left this earth. Aside from a recent conversation with one of my aunts, I didn't know what triggered my sister to run away from home during her teen years. But, to give context, she always believed our mother loved me more. Roughly a decade passed before my mother located her, and she came to live with us for a time.

I am not aware of any discussion or reconciliation that took place, but I knew my sister had not healed after my mother went to spend time with her on another island. When Mummy returned home, she was a shadow of herself. It seemed my sister had saved up her resentment and spent it on our mother in the year she'd been with her.

It's hard not to take sides, but I don't have all the details. What I do know is that shortly before she died, my mother reached out in a letter asking for forgiveness for whatever she had done that made my sister hate her so, trying to set things right. My sister did not respond. Nor did she attend the funeral. According to the family grapevine, lately, she is in touch with one or two persons. I am not one of those.

Let's jump backward to the time I was in high school. I was close with someone, who later proved to be a *frenemy*. It's amazing how the memories we suppress come back when we're ready to face them. So many incidents were clues this girl didn't like me, yet we were besties. Growing up solo, I loved company and was always seeking approval. Clearly, I was all too willing to overlook signposts that stared me in the face.

Come with me again; now, I'm older and in a work environment. I've been placed in positions of responsibility during my entire working life. I believe in operating with a spirit of excellence and getting through my tasks as quickly as possible. I've had the pleasure and privilege of working with some top-class team members and I've worked alongside mediocre employees.

It's inevitable that when excellence and mediocrity meet, there will be a difference in opinion on how things should be done. I'm not someone who believes my way is the only way to complete a job, but it irks me when I'm part of a team that's underperforming.

Something I've found with people who do the bare minimum, is that they resent those who do what's required, or go beyond what's needed. When hard workers are praised, they want to hear none of it, and have bad things to say. Never mind the fact that everyone is operating in the same environment with equal opportunity to contribute.

To backtrack a little, I was raised in a peaceful home, but there were times when my mother didn't handle the stresses of life well. On those occasions, I felt the lash of her tongue. Later in life, I recognized the same patterns when they showed up in my life.

I'd stress about something that had nothing to do with my family, and when my son interrupted me, wanting me to deal with another issue, I'd snap at him. Of course, I had to work through my bad attitude and let him know my reaction had nothing to do with him. It was challenging to unlearn that behavior and be patient with my family when work, or other stressors had me in their grip.

The Struggle

We all struggle and even in church, I've come across people with terrible interpersonal skills. God has given us hundreds of gifts and talents we don't recognize. When they are nurtured, we grow in ways we cannot predict.

I believe the church is where these God-given gifts are to be encouraged, because they are given to us to serve the community. Unfortunately, as my bestie tells me, "The same people in the world are the ones who come to church."

There's nothing wrong with that. We're all there seeking Christ. The challenge is when we make others uncomfortable in His House. I've had someone in the same ministry sit next to me and not speak with me for some time. When I expressed my opinion in group discussions, this same person acted like nothing was said. As if I didn't exist.

One Sunday morning, the pastor, who came on a "pulpit exchange" visit, said we should forget the things God has already put under our feet. While I pondered that, I heard in my spirit, *'The problem you're thinking about is already behind you.'*

I wasn't sure what it meant. If I took it literally, the words referred to the person holding the grudge who, incidentally, sat directly behind me. If I looked deeper, it meant I should give that issue to Him. After thinking about it some more, clarification came. Despite how that person chose to behave, I also had choices. I could continue to wear out my mind about the situation, or act as if I believed God was taking care of me.

That realization freed me. She wasn't putting food on my table or paying my bills, so I had no reason to be uneasy. All I needed to work on was containing my resentment and stop winding my head up in knots about what, at the root, was a personality problem.

I've learned that many of us in church don't forgive, no matter what the Bible says about the subject. I've also learned that we internalize our insecurities and they fester and grow. When dealing with people I believe have deep-seated issues, I tread gently. And at every stage of my life, when I've had disagreements with others, I ask myself:

Was I at fault?
If not directly responsible, did I contribute to the problem?

Did I handle that the right way?
Could I have done something differently?
Should I apologize?

Depending on the answers, I move accordingly. It's never easy to apologize but when you're wrong, it feels good to do so—after the fact —because you know you've done the right thing.

It is important that we recognize where we are in this journey called life, the impact we have, and the legacy we will leave behind. We may think we can't influence anyone or anything, but that's a limited view. Many of us are raising children and we're the first glimpse of society they get before they are exposed to other people.

None of us were born angry, bitter, insecure, or toxic. We allow life, society, and our personal situation to change our personality as we grow older. Before we know it, we're no longer open, we don't say what we mean, or express our feelings. We become closed in, unable to express the way we feel. With no outlet, our doubts and fears marinate and morph into harmful traits. We become people we were *not* created to be. At worst, we become toxic.

Identifying Toxicity

Toxic people are harmful to those around them, and they impact others in significant ways. So, what is toxic behavior? The term refers to our actions or attitudes that are harmful, destructive, or negative. By their negative attitude, toxic people leave others feeling drained, anxious, nervous and even depressed.

Toxicity manifests in a variety of ways, including:

- Manipulative or controlling behavior, such as trying to make others feel guilty, or using emotional blackmail to get your own way. In other words, playing mind games.
- Judgmental or critical attitudes, such as constantly belittling others.
- Playing people off against each other and sowing seeds of discord.

- Narcissistic behavior, such as constantly seeking attention or validation, or putting your own needs and desires over those of other people.
- Bullying, name-calling, and other aggressive or abusive actions, such as shouting at, or physically and emotionally abusing others.
- Blaming others by finger-pointing and refusing to take responsibility for one's own actions.
- Gaslighting, which is emotional manipulation in which the perpetrator denies the realness of their victim's experience, which makes them question their sanity.
- Locking individuals out of social groups by badmouthing them.
- Spreading rumors and gossip with the aim of destroying someone's reputation.

All of these patterns are damaging to those who are constantly around the toxic person, and make it difficult, or impossible, for them to maintain healthy relationships or feel confident and secure in themselves.

There are a variety of reasons people exhibit toxic behavior, but the way they function may be the result of learned behavior. If they were raised in an environment where they were routinely criticized, and their home life was filled with arguments and recurring conflict, they may not know any other way to communicate.

Other reasons for this kind of behavior may be because of:

- Insecurity or low self-esteem: Some people feel the need to put others down or control them in order to feel better about themselves. They may be afraid of rejection or abandonment, and try to manipulate or control others to avoid dealing with their feelings.
- Trauma or past experiences: People who have experienced trauma or abuse in the past may be more likely to exhibit toxicity, as they may have learned their modus operandi from their abuser/s.

- Mental health issues: Certain mental health conditions, such as narcissistic personality disorder, can lead to toxic displays. People with these disorders may struggle to identify with others, or be considerate of other people.

Looking Yourself in the Eyes

No matter the reason, toxic behavior is never acceptable. If you recognize that you are acting in a toxic way, it's important to face who you have become and deal with your shortcomings. Some critical steps will be to:

1. Recognize your faults: The first step to changing any bad habit is to recognize that it's a problem. Take some time to reflect on your actions and how they are affecting those around you. Be honest with yourself about the impact you've had on others.

2. Take responsibility: Once you've recognized your behavior, it's important to take responsibility for it. Don't make excuses or blame others. Own up to what you've been doing and commit to making a change.

3. Seek help: Changing toxic behavior can be difficult, and it's important to seek help if you need it. This might mean talking to a therapist or counselor. In Jamaica, most people do not seek help for mental issues, but for those who opt not to see a professional, friends and family can be a tremendous source of support.

4. Practice empathy: Toxic behavior often stems from a lack of empathy for others. Practice putting yourself in other people's shoes and understanding their perspective.

5. Set boundaries: If you tend to be controlling or manipulative, it's important to learn to respect other people's boundaries. This means accepting that others have their own needs and desires, and learning to compromise.

FROM STUCK TO LIMITLESS   83

6. Practice self-care: Finally, it's important to practice self-care. Toxic behavior can be a sign of underlying issues, and taking care of yourself can help address these issues. This might mean getting enough sleep, eating well, and engaging in activities that make you happy.

Dealing With Toxicity in Others

If you're dealing with a toxic person, it's important to protect yourself and set boundaries. Equally, if you're the one exhibiting toxic behavior, remember it's not healthy or productive, and can have serious negative consequences for you and those who live and work with you.

If the person exhibiting this kind of unhealthy behavior is close to you, find a gentle way to let them know how they're affecting others. Of course, it's important that they understand you're not making accusations, but trying to help them recognize how their attitude has become problematic. If they listen, the next step is finding ways to make a 360° shift.

So how can toxic people change the way they act and become more positive and supportive? There are a variety of methods that can be effective, depending on the individual and their specific situation. Some crucial steps include:

Therapy: Therapy is a helpful tool. A skilled therapist can help them explore the underlying reasons for their behavior, identify patterns and triggers, and develop healthier coping mechanisms and ways to communicate.

Self-reflection: Often, toxicity is driven by unconscious patterns and beliefs. By taking the time to reflect on the things they do and how their actions affect others, a toxic person can pinpoint these patterns and make changes.

Mindfulness: Practicing mindfulness can help a toxic person become more aware of their thoughts, feelings, and deeds in each moment. Being 'present' can help them identify when they are exhibiting toxic behavior and take steps to shift in a positive direction.

Skill-building: It's important for a toxic person to develop new skills and strategies for interacting with others. This might include learning how to communicate more effectively, taking time out to reflect before responding to situations that may be triggering, while allowing themselves grace as they learn better coping skills.

Social support: Having supportive friends or family members who provide encouragement and accountability is helpful. Joining a support group or seeking a mentor or coach are also good ways to make permanent changes.

Despite the mistakes I have made and how others have made me feel, I've learned that I'm no more important than the next person, and they are no more important than I am.

I've wasted time internalizing unkind words that were said to, and about, me. I've let them wound my spirit, while wondering what I did to deserve that kind of venom. It took me years to realize that despite the façade we wear, what's inside of us will eventually show out. I've made peace with the fact that some of what has been said about me had nothing to do with me, but with other people's unresolved internal struggles.

We can only do better if we're committed to the process of changing. And we have to show up each and every day, willing to work for the results we want to see manifested in our lives.

I've learned to give grace to those who have not yet started the work of acknowledging and releasing toxicity, and I'm grateful I've not allowed the toxins released in my direction to poison my soul.

I'm that much stronger for dealing with the personalities and relationships that have not served me well. Most of all, I thank God for giving me strength to endure, keeping me under the shadow of His wings, and always providing me with *a word in due season*.

18 "Do not remember the former things,
   Nor consider the things of old.
   19 Behold, I will do a new thing,

Now it shall spring forth;
Shall you not know it?
I will even make a road in the wilderness
And rivers in the desert.
20 The beast of the field will honor Me,
The jackals and the ostriches,
Because I give waters in the wilderness
And rivers in the desert,
To give drink to My people, My chosen.
21 This people I have formed for Myself;
They shall declare My praise.
Isaiah 43:18-21 (New King James Version)

Thanks to Him, I'm better, not bitter.

Selah.
J.L. Campbell

ABOUT J.L. CAMPBELL

NATIONAL BESTSELLING AUTHOR, J.L. Campbell writes contemporary, paranormal, and sweet romance, romantic suspense, women's fiction, as well as new and young adult novels.

Campbell, who features Jamaican culture in her stories, has penned over forty books. She is a certified editor, workshop presenter, and book coach. When she's not writing, Campbell adds to her extensive collection of photos detailing Jamaica's flora and fauna. Visit her on the web at www.joylcampbell.com

Follow J.L. on Social Media:
https://sociatap.com/JL_Campbell/

VANESSA

Trauma does not define the beauty of your soul. Recovering from incest can be a long and painful journey. I've evicted the ghost from my past and embraced a brighter future. The melodies from my renewed heart sing a new song because I am a stronger person.

CHAPTER 9
SOULFUL SOUNDS FROM A ONCE BROKEN SPIRIT

THE RUNT in a bunch of seven children should feel protected, especially if she's the youngest, and the only girl. My story is no different from other American women because one out of six have potentially been the victim of an attempted, or completed, rape in her lifetime. My abuser happened to live with me, and he was my older brother.

Defenseless

Tick, tock. Tick, tock was the only reminder that time was not standing still. My mind focused on the steady sound of the clock to provide a needed diversion from what my abuser was doing to my fragile frame. So many times, I wanted to yell, "Get off me!"

My words were silenced by the agony I experienced while listening to my abuser's shallow breathing and smelling his disgusting, rank breath.

He was a diabolical abuser that did his deed in the presence of my other brothers. No one noticed that I was always the partner he selected to play childhood games of hide-and-seek or building forts with sheets. I always wondered if anyone heard the sounds he made as he touched me, or my muffled cries as he forcibly silenced me with his large hand clamped over my mouth. Who could have imagined that simple childhood games would cause me to remain in a state of hypervigilance and carrying suppressed memories for decades?

My abuser was over ten years older than me and had a roster of girlfriends who catered to his sexual needs. I was the warm-up act that helped him develop his sexual prowess, even though young ladies who he wasn't related to were willing to oblige his primal cravings. He was a ladies' man—tall, dark and handsome, as I was told by his admirers. Teenage girls befriended me frequently to get close to him. In the summertime, when my parents were at work, girls would come to the house for heavy petting sessions with him. Sometimes, my other brothers and I watched his sexual escapades with these young ladies from the stairwell.

I was his special playmate and like all *Playboy Bunnies*, I was paid for my silence. In this case, it was with candy. No one would ever believe that as we built forts in our bunkbeds with sheets and blankets to create rooms, this pervert was doing unspeakable things to my body.

He was a smooth criminal in every sense of the word, because he knew how to deflect his devious deeds, mistreating me in the presence of my siblings. There were times when he locked me in the closet for hours to show my other brothers that he had a great disdain for me. He called me horrible names and said I was a snitch, so my other brothers excluded me from family play times.

While we're supposed to be playing, my abuser did unmentionable things to me. I winced in pain and tears rolled down the side of my face each time he abused me. He shoved his massive hand over my tiny mouth. Then he'd whisper in my ear, "Shh. I'll stop. This is our secret. If you tell Daddy, he is going to kill you for letting me do this to you." While the excruciating pain engulfed my defenseless body, our siblings played gleefully with each other in the same room, not knowing the horror that was happening to their baby sister.

I tried desperately to remove his smell from my body by washing frequently, changing my underwear, and wiping excessively after each bathroom visit. But these coping mechanisms were in vain.

When he went away to college, I was happy. His absence from the home was my saving grace, allowing me to forget his violations to my body.

My abuser was very athletic, winning many awards and trophies for his speed in track and the ability to knock opponents down in boxing. I didn't have to see him on a daily basis to be reminded of his sexual advances and it didn't surprise me that a woman on campus accused him of rape. He lost his scholarship. I was eternally grateful my dad didn't allow him to come back home to live with us.

Family and friends often advise me to forgive him and move on. It is not that I haven't forgiven him. I'm not safe around him. My brother was diagnosed with mental illness and has been hospitalized because he brought harm to himself or someone else. His psychologist warned me sternly, "I could lose my job for telling you this. Never be in a room alone with your brother because he wants to hurt you. I can't share with you the things he said because of patient confidentiality, however, don't go around your brother anymore."

Needless to say, we do not have any communication or contact.

He attempted to abuse me again on two occasions. One time in my twenties, and the last in my fifties. Last year, my cousin died, and I was spending time with the family. My brother walked into my aunt's house and didn't recognize me.

Slowly, I gathered my things and tried to make a quick exit, as my aunt said, "Bye, Van. It was good to see you."

I walked faster toward the black, steel security door.

My brother, asked, "Is that my sister?"

The family confirmed that it was me.

I rushed through the hallway to the door and closed it behind me. He opened it and grabbed my arm, attempting to drag me back into the house, then growled, "Get your ass back inside. Stop running from me."

My arms trembled and I shook as he held onto me. I was transformed into little scared Vanessa as I tried to escape his strong grip. I gathered all the strength I could muster, snatched my arm away, and slid down the steps away from him.

"What have I done to you?" he yelled.

I looked defiantly at him, glaring and daring him to make one more move closer to me. "You know what you did to me," I responded.

Then, I ran across the street to where my female cousin stood.

He walked along the sidewalk staring at us with fireworks in his eyes. This was the first time we had a witness to how violently he treated his sister. After he skulked back into the house, I went home.

I couldn't get his touch and smell off my mind and body. At this point, I'd disclosed the abuse to my family. I called two of my older brothers and told them what happened, hoping that finally someone would protect me from this demon. I was certain my brothers would do great bodily harm to this pervert to make up for the times they didn't protect me. I kept waiting for their response and when it came, I was beyond disappointed.

It wasn't until I shared my story with a female sexual trauma survivor that I reached a new resolve for dealing with his assault. It was time to call the police, get a restraining order, and have him arrested.

One of my brothers asked me to wait and let him have a conversation with the abuser first. That talk occurred a week or two later.

In the meantime, I was triggered, depressed, and bedbound—reliving the new and old trauma. My 'Nightmare on Elm Street' wouldn't let me sleep. I was haunted by his touch and his venomous words played over and over in my head.

The resolution of my brother's conversation with *him* was that if I wanted to visit with the family, I was to call one of my brothers and they would go with me.

Wow! I was speechless and disappointed once more.

From this point forward, my security and safety were up to me. The police *would* be called, and I *would* press charges against this sexual predator.

Broken Pieces

I repressed the memories of my abuse for many years. My trauma manifested itself through fear, dressing to minimize attention, nightmares, jitters, anxiety, bed-wetting, and demanding extreme privacy when changing my clothes. At times, I was overly obedient to authority figures because I lacked confidence.

Depression and low self-esteem became my middle name because I was ashamed and felt guilty. Withdrawal from friends and family became my norm, which led to me overeating, and weighing over two hundred and fifty pounds.

The abuse directly affected my growing brain. I struggled with trust and began to overcompensate for the loss of control in my life by striving for perfection, overeating, excessively washing myself, avoiding social interactions, making emotional decisions, and I was easily startled.

I learned early to keep a smile in place and stay silent. My pleasant façade masked the sadness I carried inside. It hid my inner turmoil. My silence kept the family secret from being exposed.

Soulful Sounds Rebound

Keeping secrets carries emotional, mental, physical, and spiritual impact. Your thoughts set the direction for every day and every single aspect of your life. Our thoughts create feelings, which influence our actions. We become what we think.

In order to sing, you have to practice. I had to retrain my brain to think differently and learn better ways to live my life without being bound by fear. I needed to create new muscle memories of a holistic, well-rounded person. So, I had to be intentional in my habits, thoughts, and actions to create new conscious pathways using coping mechanisms. Here are a few adjustments I made to recalibrate my life.

Music: In the Bible, when Saul was vexed with an evil spirit, he sent for David to play music. Music has always been one of the tools I use to transform disposition. Listening to music increases the blood flow to the brain region that generates and controls our emotions. When listening to your favorite melodies, dopamine is released and activates the brain's pleasure and reward system. For me, music has an immediate positive effect on mood by energizing and recentering me.

I have created a playlist to positively affect my mood and energy. Research shows that happy, upbeat music helps the brain produce chemicals like dopamine and serotonin to evoke feelings of joy, and calming music relaxes the mind and body. Music increases the blood flow to the brain regions that generate and control emotions.

Writing: I journal to help me unpack my deep, emotional traumas that are difficult to share with others. Writing helps me to process my feelings. I can privately put pen to paper and recount my thoughts and feelings in a safe space. I use color markers, stickers, Post-It notes, and sketches as a creative outlet to provide an opportunity for positive self-talk to minimize negative patterns. Journaling also helps me to keep track of triggers and learn ways to better control them.

Exercising: I try to start my day off walking on my treadmill. Exercising helps our nervous system restore balance by burning adrenaline and releasing endorphins through movement. Endorphins help combat situational depression. When I am working from home, periodically, I will jump on the trampoline to refocus myself.

Hydration: I drink alkaline water because it neutralizes the acid in my blood stream. Research has linked dehydration to depression and anxiety. Our mental health is driven primarily by our brain's activity. When we are dehydrated, our brain function slows down.

Self-Care: I do things to take care of myself so I can stay physically, spiritually, mentally, and emotionally well. My sleeping habits are getting better. I'm eating healthier, exercising, spending time with friends, and gardening. I ensure that my focus is on doing things that make me happy and healthy.

Therapy: Although my abuse happened many years ago, because I didn't formally address my trauma, triggers occurred that made me relive the sense of hopelessness I had as a child. I started therapy after my divorce and focused on healing and putting my life back together. It was not easy sharing that part of my life with others. When I confronted my brother as an adult, he yelled vehemently at me like a spitting devil with his foul breath, "Yes, I did it. Get over it. Life goes on. I wasn't trying to hurt you. I was hurting your father since you were the closest thing to him."

My therapist has given me tools to notice triggers, cope with anxiety, and develop effective ways to deal with my emotions. I recently wrote an impact statement about my traumatic upbringing. The goal of writing an impact statement was for me to describe the personal meaning of the traumatic events and how they have affected my view of myself, other people, and the world. I felt empowered with the understanding that mental illness was one of the factors that led to my abuse. My former negative views of myself have been dispelled. I transformed those thoughts into positive affirmations:

I am a beautiful woman
I can stop eating when I am full
I can trust people with my emotions
I can give up control
I can receive and give love
I can create my own safe bubble
I can trust others to help me

My mantra is posted on my mirror in my bathroom, "You are worthy."

1) Accept love that is given
2) Receive kindness with grace
3) You are qualified and deserve a seat at the table
4) You are a fearless and wonderfully made child of God
5) You are a queen, deserving a king.

My therapist provides a safe place for me to talk through my life challenges and reteach my brain to look at situations differently. Getting guidance from friends and family is good, however, if you want to be the best version of yourself, seek professional assistance.

Therapists are trained to assist with resolving concerns and behavior patterns in our lives. If I had a throbbing tooth that needed to be pulled, I would go to the dentist to get relief, not tell my friend.

I've done the work and have evicted the ghost from my past, to embrace a brighter future. My life is not perfect, but I am becoming the best version of myself using the tools I've learned.

You can, too.

Dr. Vanessa Howard

ABOUT DR. VANESSA HOWARD

DR. VANESSA HOWARD, affectionately known as Dr. V, is an award-winning educator and #1 Bestselling author with her debut memoir, "From the Projects to a Ph.D."

Dr. V. first put pen to paper by writing high-interest stories for her students, using authentic experiences they loved to read. Her motto is, "Discover Life, Literacy, and Legacy with Dr. V." All elements can be found in her body of work, which includes children's, Christian, women's fiction, and non-fiction books that focus on relationships.

. . .

96 MARIE MCKENZIE

Follow Dr. V. on Social Media:

Facebook: https://www.facebook.com/drvhoward
Instagram: https://www.instagram.com/drvhoward/
Twitter: https://twitter.com/DrVanessaHowar1
Website: https://www.howarducity.com

PAT

Sailing on this wobbly ship called, My Life I encountered rough weather, experiences that made Hell seem as cold as Winter. Anxious perspiration was my constant companion while I gripped the mental and physical helm for what seemed an eternity.

I would liken that experience to one similar to the Apostle Paul as he sailed to Rome. While his ship hurled about and he was discouraged by the ship's captain to turn back, he didn't listen. That was me on so many occasions. I was discouraged by those who thought they were helping. Instead, I discarded unnecessary baggage that could've caused my life to spiral out of control and miss God's purpose for it.

And, like Paul, who with God's protection and his faith made it successfully to shore while clinging to splinters of his ship, he ultimately built a fire that warmed the other survivors. I, too, survived— albeit on "Broken Pieces" to write many bestsellers which warmed hearts with humor.

CHAPTER 10
ON BROKEN PIECES

THE FIRST TWENTY-FIVE Years

Paul said to the centurion and the soldiers,
"Except these abide in the ship, ye cannot be saved."
Acts: 27:31 (King James Version)

As I sailed through many storms during my seventy-five-year life voyage, this passage of scripture became clear and more meaningful. It is my Providence life raft. From birth up to my twenty-fifth year, I've christened "the Wobbly."

Why?

Through storm after storm, swelling waters of controversies attacked my life. One of my first memories was a rescue. I was six years old when I was pulled from a raging fire by a brave fireman who crammed my small body under his coat. I remember the heat, the screams, the chorus of outside voices yelling, "Mother, come out," as the man I later came to learn named John O'Donnell, carried me through a wall of flames in Mount Vernon, New York.

FROM STUCK TO LIMITLESS   99

That rescue was short-lived, as my Life Ship continued its struggle to reach a welcoming shore, lost without a compass.

From the time my mother left my sister, and I, supposedly in the safekeeping of our maternal grandmother, my nine-year-old mind grappled to understand boundaries—particularly familial ones.

I was always a smart student in my New York schools, and so entering the Southern school system should have been a smooth transition. It didn't work that way. Without school records or transfer papers, I was placed in a third-grade class that was right for my age.

My third-grade teacher, Miss Bobbie Madison saw my capabilities and fought to place me in the proper fourth grade. I later learned she'd also seen signs that something wasn't quite right in the way I presented myself. I was smart, but also very timid. Sometimes very talkative but with imaginary people that were always happy but in dire situations. She allowed me to follow her around while the other children were at recess and entertain her with my ridiculous stories.

Little did she know how close to reality her sense of foreboding had been. During the times that I attached myself to Miss Madison I was enduring relentless sexual molestation from my Southern uncle. Right under the noses of my grandparents and other family members, he terrorized me from the age of nine through twelve. I tried telling on him one time and received a severe beating because the consensus was that "New York kids lie." It left him free to not only abuse me, but I discovered later that I wasn't the only one. He delighted in abusing his young nieces.

I can't say I was happy he died a horrible death later in life. I also can't say that I wasn't.

Many years later, when I became a National Bestselling Author, Miss Madison would tell me with her beautiful smile on display, "Patricia, I always knew you would be a writer because you were the biggest liar I had in the third grade."

Back to my voyage on the Life Ship.

When my maternal grandfather died, my mother arrived from New York to attend his funeral. I was still naïve and believed she'd take my sister and me back to New York. We were only supposed to be with my grandparents for the summer, and I'd seen four summers already.

She left the morning after the funeral. There were no goodbyes, neither from her nor my younger sister who she'd taken with her.

Another piece of my Life Ship left with her, and the ocean became torturous.

I needed an escape or rescue. My mental state of denial was not viable. I was stuck.

And then as if my life had screamed to the Universe, "Hold my beer. She ain't seen or suffered enough," I began to accept the role of being stuck in whatever situation came my way. What was the point of fighting?

———

My grandmother relocated to St. Augustine, Florida to live with one of her other daughters but she didn't take me.

At that time, my mother was off the radar for several years, It didn't take long before my spirit devolved into another broken piece. I was twelve and placed in Foster Care. I eventually landed in New York to live with my father, stepmother, and four siblings in Mount Vernon, New York where I'd been born. My stepmother announced on the day of my arrival, she would never accept me and for the next four years, she kept her word.

My refuge, as always, was school and when I graduated from Junior High School with excellent grades, it was no surprise.

Barely a month later after graduation, I was attacked and raped by a man in military uniform and left to die in a Bronx, New York wooded area on my way back from a wedding. That harrowing experience came with the usual disappointment in adults who should've protected me.

But, me being discovered bloody and dazed was a condition that embarrassed my father. His response was, "It was late. She should've had someone walk her home."

The fact was, my best friend's father got drunk at her brother's wedding reception and couldn't escort me home. I'd walked those twenty blocks often without problems, but never in the dark. My father concluded it was better not to report the assault.

FROM STUCK TO LIMITLESS   101

Stuck and struck again.

My only solace, after not receiving medical attention and laying with a pillow under my buttocks for comfort, came several weeks later. It seemed that not everyone in my family was willing to let the violation go. Retribution was meted out by another military family member, who found the perpetrator. I will leave it at that.

———

Throughout my teen years and into my twenties, I'd come close to being happy only to have my Life Ship hit tidal waves of disappointment.

There were moments of respite—brief but certainly welcomed.

In my early twenties I'd come to accept that breakers of near misses, controversies, and periods of peace whittled my self-esteem to street curb level. I decided to leave it to providence to decide whether I'd make it. If God wanted me to survive, despite all I continued to go through, He needed to show up and show out.

Although, I left it up to God, I admit there were temporary thoughts of suicide along with my devotion to Him. The strange thing was that although both of my parents had separated and remarried, somehow along the way, they became preachers and pastors. Mom was Pentecostal and Dad was Baptist.

Go figure.

Age Twenty-Six to Fifty

Like the frightened passengers on Paul's ship, leaving my well-being to Providence meant giving up some things in order not to drown.

I'd gone through having a church I attended order me to marry a man I'd known for three days. The fact that he'd leave to fight a war in the next two weeks didn't seem to be an issue. It certainly became one when he unknowingly left me pregnant.

A year later, he returned. Of course, that marriage was doomed. We didn't know each other before he left and what little I knew of him didn't resemble the man who returned.

After five years of spousal abuse, I still held onto my Salvation, but it needed to include me saving myself and now three children.

I leaned over the deck of my soul and hurled overboard anything to lighten my load and secure mental and physical survival. I courageously abandoned people, places, and things. When I finally took a moment to breathe, reality came at dawn instead of the sun. Each discarded piece took a part of my Life Ship with it—until nothing was left but splinters.

I was reminded of God's Providence.

Each splinter from my Life Ship was strong enough to carry me to a successful shore.

For example, the time I spent in the entertainment industry, both on and off the stage, in hindsight was a part of Providence—becoming unstuck and surviving on the broken pieces of life. I also felt guilty because of the times I spent apart from my children and my second husband, Rob.

It was a hard choice. Deciding to do what I believed would make me happy, but happy enough to make them see it, too, wasn't easy. However delusional that thought, it didn't take long before repercussions nipped away at my family.

I never figured that becoming unstuck would be a part of Providence. Instead, I faced the frequent demands from an industry that commanded nothing less than one hundred percent of my being, my time, or the anger that often consumed me. I'd agonize when I took action that went against my morals or beliefs. With each occasion, it was as though flood waters entered my ship.

Every time I wanted to quit, I couldn't. My pride at being honored or recognized in such a competitive industry wouldn't let me. I'd remember the conversations with my mother when things got tough, and my life felt as though I was constantly peeling away a scab that covered an unhealed wound.

She'd often tell me, "Look, stand still. You stay on this ship just like the Apostle Paul did when he went on God's mission without a clue. He had only one ship. You have only one life and so you be like Paul.

His ship came apart little by little. If he made it on broken pieces, so can you. We serve the same God. He's processing you into a piece of Black steel."

I am my mother's daughter and so like her, I needed to stay on this Life Ship until I reached wherever the shore was. However, God's providential method would get me there.

I tried my best to remain my mother's daughter in thought and in deed. I didn't always succeed. Apparently, God's plan for me becoming unlimited was shrouded in mystery. He was keeping a secret.

In the mid-nineties, a huge, unexpected wave tossed my Life Ship like it was a paper boat. I had to leave the industry that gave me headaches and my popularity. I wasn't going to be as happy as Paul when he reached the safety of the shore, I braced myself. What else could I do?

Age 50+ Now What?

Along with my severance check with almost seven figures, came a reality check with zero dollars.

I'd gone from complaining and feeling stuck in the recording industry, to stagnation in life.

What was I to do with all that experience I'd fought against gaining, and often being complicit in achieving success by any means, good or bad?

I was fifty years old. What could I do at this age? I wasn't like Grandma Moses, who began painting at the age of one hundred; I could draw stick people and great flowers, but that wouldn't work.

Seated in my car in a Walmart's parking lot, I suddenly remembered another conversation with my mother.

"Are you ever satisfied?" she'd asked me. "You wanted a break. You got a break. Be a Pauline if you can't be a Paul. What are you, a one-act? Find something else."

Like what?

Writing was something I'd done for my own pleasure, and among my collection were a few monologues. Those short pieces came in handy for a church fund-raising, or a pastor's appreciation, and anniversary programs.

I performed my monologues while dressed in an outrageous costume that included the ugliest hat I found at Sears Department store, a bedazzled gold cross, a mind-dizzying colored apron, and a fan that featured a picture of me.

Those moments were comedic, and they told a satiric story of a crazy and egocentric, elderly church lady. She's home one day watching her soap operas when she receives a telephone call from Jesus. He says he's stopping by for a chat, but in her excitement she hangs up before he finishes speaking. She has her own interpretation of what he was trying to tell her. Why would Jesus visit if he didn't need her opinion on Salvation and its ins and outs?

In my portrayal of the character, Sister Betty, like many Christians thought more highly of herself than she should. In a comedic way, I demonstrated the familiar, unchristian-like manner known to many.

Her behavior was that of someone thinking she must have earned a seat on the other side of Jesus with God leaning in her direction first.

Although my *Sister Betty, God's Calling You* one-woman skit was popular, and I was paid, the one thing I wasn't—was happy. I still struggled to become unstuck.

Was this my limit?

From Stuck to Unlimited

One day I happened to chat with LaJoyce Birkshire. She was the author of the Bestselling novel, *Soul Food*, and it set in motion the Providence God had placed on my life.

We'd become friends when she was a publicist at Arista Records, and I was in Promotion and Marketing at Columbia and Def Jam Records.

LaJoyce sternly told me to stop whining and find something I liked doing. We'd both taken a writing course some time back in New York City, and she was aware of my other interest, as well as trying to put to paper my Sister Betty stories.

"Write one of those crazy church lady stories," she said.

FROM STUCK TO LIMITLESS   105

Of course, that wave called Doubt came rushing at me. Despite LaJoyce's suggestion, that shore seemed farther out of sight.

My thinking was: who would care about a little old church lady who thought she was God's right-hand gal on earth? Who would give a second thought to an angel who got into Heaven on a technicality and couldn't get his wings until he helped that old church lady. And certainly, who would waste time reading about a congregation of misfits pastored by a man (Rev. Knott Enuff Money) who needed Jesus more than those to whom he preached?

And that's when I created the Ain't Nobody Right But Us—All Others Goin' to Hell church. I went on to create a tagline: *Don't let worry kill ya off. Let the Church help.*

I didn't have a clue about publishing, but what I did have was all the skills I'd fought against during the years in the recording industry while promoting and marketing artists such as Regina Belle, Michael Bolton, New Kids on the Block, Public Enemy, LL Cool J, and many others to success.

As if I were preparing to promote an album from which I would select first a single, and release it to the public, I took one of my short stories and treated it the same. In my mind, the audience that liked music couldn't be different from those who liked to read. After all, I loved music and reading. It shouldn't be that hard.

I didn't know I wasn't supposed to do that. No thought given to who would be interested in a twenty-two-page book/pamphlet with a staple in the center of its spine.

Ignorance is bliss is how the saying goes. I was past bliss; I dove right into the publishing waters without a clue, and didn't have the sense not to do everything I was doing.

God's Providence took off running. Using the internet as my launching tool, along with videos from my performances, my Sister Betty Gospel Comedy series launched.

What lay ahead defied limits.

Small books without a spine or less than fifty pages, with a staple in its middle, were deemed pamphlets. The subject of church satire wasn't a thing. Going from performing in local churches to performing on cruise ships, large theatres, mega churches, television, a great number of book clubs—among other venues and groups—took over my life. Each successful step landed me on the shores of success, buoyed by splinters of the broken pieces of my life.

Being given a chance by Kensington Books' new Imprint, Dafina, was the defining moment. They took all seven of my short stories and released them in a collection titled, *Sister Betty! God's Calling You, Again.*

It was followed by ten other novels, of which two landed on the Essence Bestsellers List as well as the National Bestsellers List, and all are available on audio and in mass market, soft cover, and in e-book formats.

Sister Betty and her assorted church nuttz garnered several Publishers Weekly starred reviews, as well as the coronation of being the creator of what became known as Gospel Comedy.

Finally, I went From Stuck to Limitless and so far, remain.

I give thanks to God, my publishing company, editors, all my readers, and the Apostle Paul.

Like Paul, who never gave up and arrived safely onshore, aboard many broken pieces, my Life Ship turned into a voyage from broken to limitless.

Pat G'Orge-Walker

ABOUT PAT G'ORGE-WALKER

PAT G'ORGE-WALKER, National and Essence Bestselling author, creator of the Award-winning Sister Betty series, Fire in the Water, Somewhat Saved, Choices, more than fifteen books, and Ebooks, published by Kensington/Dafina and Macron resides in North Carolina.

Follow Pat on Social Media:
https://bit.ly/sociatappgwalker

ANN

It's commonplace to hear about people using drugs or alcohol to assuage pain and trauma. Their stories of triumph often inspire others to turn away from addictive substances and habits. But what do you do when your drug of choice is food, which is necessary for survival? If you use unhealthy foods to self-medicate and blunt the pain and mental anguish of past or current circumstances, deliverance and healing awaits you through Christ!

CHAPTER 11

EXODUS FROM THE WILDERNESS OF OBESITY TO CLAIM THE PROMISED LAND OF HEALTHY AND FIT FOR LIFE

LIKE MANY PEOPLE, my weight has fluctuated for most of my life. At puberty, I leveled off, and the weight went to all the right places. However, that changed when I went to college. For some unknown reason, all of my old childhood demons resurfaced during my sophomore year after I had met and fallen in love with the man who would eventually become my husband.

In my very biased opinion, Andre was, and still is, perfect, and he loved very imperfect me. Since my self-esteem was almost non-existent at that time, I could not imagine why he loved me, so it should come as no surprise that I constantly worried, "If only he knew that …"

… I was sexually abused by an uncle *and* an aunt. I wondered, *will he still want me?*

… I had struggled with bouts of clinical depression, which required medication since I was in the 5th grade. I was afraid, *he'll think I'm mentally and emotionally unstable.*

… I almost believed the people who called me crazy because I was prone to fits of uncontrollable crying in class, due to the depression. I worried, *will he think I'm crazy, too?*

... I was mercilessly teased and bullied as a kid because very few classmates ever really liked me. I was concerned that, *he'll think I'm not worthy of his love either.*

... I felt that I deserved the bullying because I believed my tormentors when they called me ugly. I was scared that, *he'll stop finding me attractive if he knew that.*

... At one point, the teasing and physical assaults were so bad that I stood in my parents' kitchen in the middle of the night, holding a steak knife to my chest with tears streaming down my face, trying to work up the courage to push it through. I was convinced, *he'll think I'm a suicidal nut who is not worth the risk, and break up with me.*

Fortunately, I could not plunge the knife into my chest because even as a child, God's *still, small voice* spoke to my troubled spirit and promised me that things would get better (1 Kings 19:12). I did not completely understand it then, but for some reason, I chose to believe the comforting voice and went back to bed.

Although the change was not immediate, things did get better over time. Eventually, I made some true friends, one of whom is still my best friend to this day. Consequently, it was mind-boggling that when I thought I had put all of that behind me, the episodes of physical assaults and sexual abuse played in my head like a CD on repeat.

The memories made me so sad that I slipped backward into depression. As a result, I started taking medication again to rid myself of the miserable thoughts. In addition to that, I followed the suggestion I heard on a popular talk show at the time, to write about unpleasant past experiences in a journal.

One night while my future husband was studying, I cried as I wrote about a particularly brutal assault, where the classroom bully made every kid in the class take a turn hitting me while the teacher was out of the room.

When Andre noticed me crying, I finally told him about the nagging thoughts and confided everything I had endured. Thankfully, he did not suddenly hate me. On the contrary, he was compassionate and kind.

Although sharing my thoughts with him and learning that he truly did love me for me instead of superficial reasons was a great relief, it was short-lived. This was because for weeks I had already given the evil spirit of fear all the room it needed to wreak havoc in my life.

Consequently, the unpleasant trips down memory lane returned, so I decided to sign up for therapy at the university we were attending. I met a therapist who told me exactly what I wanted to hear at the time. After I explained that I did not want to think about, write about, or explore my feelings about any of the things that happened to me as a child, she shockingly agreed with me and simply said, "Then don't."

She went on to express her viewpoint that those methods were often harmful and unnecessary to get beyond painful issues that occurred in the past. I wholeheartedly agreed with her and promptly stopped writing in the journal and going to therapy. I ate instead.

I am *not* blaming the therapist. I still completely agree with her that those methods are not for everyone, and they certainly were not for me. I had already gained my *freshmen fifteen* and had been working out to lose it, which was how my husband first noticed me all those years ago.

It became easier to take the pills for the depression and drown the hurt and pain in pizza, cheeseburgers, cakes, and pies. Unfortunately, it worked. After a while, I did not think about the painful memories all the time, although they invaded my thoughts every now and then. It is no coincidence those times corresponded with the instances when I was serious about dieting.

Needless to say, it was not long before I surpassed the *freshmen fifteen*, and my svelte size eight that initially caught my husband's eye ballooned into double digit sizes.

This brought about new fears concerning our relationship. Now I worried, *will he stop being attracted to me? Is he going to leave me?* Not only did he stay, but he also married me when I was a size fourteen, proving that he loved what was within not just the outer shell. Furthermore, he stood by me and encouraged me throughout the entire decade that I rode the diet roller coaster.

FROM STUCK TO LIMITLESS 113

He was there for the high points, where through diet and exercise, I managed to make it back down to a size ten for a *very* brief period of time because I thought I could return to my old eating habits once I had lost the weight. He was also there for my lowest point, where I topped out at 269 pounds while pregnant with our first child because I thought pregnancy equated to nine months of bingeing. Unfortunately, he also joined me for the ride at some point, and it has been painful watching him endure the same unnecessary consequences.

The good news is, the Lord revealed Satan's falsehoods about my husband leaving me for the lies they were, and we are still together. The even better news is that although my husband was there to encourage and love me through it all, my God was also there. As close as my husband was to the situation, only God knew my pain intimately, and He comforted and loved me best and most of all. Only God knew ...

... I had given up one of my favorite pastimes, shopping, because I cried in the fitting rooms when the clothes did not fit.

... The emotional pain I felt when I heard about a rumor circulating at the university that I must have had an abortion because I had gained a significant amount of weight but did not have a baby to show for it nine months later.

... I would go to a buffet alone because I did not want anyone who knew me to see how much I ate, or how quickly I consumed my food.

Only God constantly and lovingly talked to me about my problem. Most importantly, only God gave me the solution to fix it. Deliverance came one night after I failed on another diet. I did not just fall off the wagon, it was more the equivalent of jumping off a plane without a parachute.

I was crying while I sat at home eating two large pizzas with cheese sticks, cinnamon sticks, and a two-liter soda. I could not stop myself, and I hated myself for it. Consequently, I did what I always do when I have done everything in my power to succeed, but continue to fail. I prayed. With tears streaming down my face, I told God I could not stop no matter how much I wanted to, and if He did not help me, I would continue to eat myself into an early grave.

During that decade of misery and self-indulgence, I truly had tried everything within my price range to lose the weight, and was on the verge of giving up completely. For instance, I tried to be a vegan, but even with exercise I only lost a few pounds.

I had my ears stapled by a chiropractor, but my appetite was only dulled for a couple of weeks. I went to a doctor who prescribed Fen-Phen diet pills like candy. Thankfully, I did not sustain heart damage like many other people did. By far, the craziest and probably the stupidest thing I did was visit a hypnotist to hypnotize me into adopting a healthier lifestyle. Needless to say, that failed, too.

I did not feel any different after I prayed. In fact, after I finished crying, I was more than willing to return to my old ways. As a result, I did not want to hear it when God began to speak to me—through His Holy Word, Bible study classes, and Sunday morning worship—about my weight and eating habits.

Where other parishioners heard sermons about freedom from sins, such as sexual immorality, or lessons on how to be good stewards over what the Lord had given them, the Holy Spirit consistently applied sermons and other Christian educational resources to the issue concerning my unhealthy diet and excess weight.

For example, during a Bible study lesson about Israel rebuilding the damaged temple and the walls surrounding Jerusalem, the Holy Spirit revealed to me that the temple and walls reflected my current spiritual condition.

Specifically, I had left my body, which is the temple of the Holy Spirit, in disrepair. It dawned on me that since God was clearly not pleased with the Israelites for their neglect of a man-made building He referred to as *His house*, how much more displeased must He be with my neglect of my body which He referred to as the "temple of the Holy Spirit" (1 Corinthians 6:19-20)?

In addition to the neglect of God's spiritual temple, the Holy Spirit also pointed out I had left myself vulnerable to the attacks of the enemy by not shielding my mind from the lies of the world's system. Because my mind had not been transformed by God's Word regarding health and fitness, it was the same as Israel leaving the city walls of Jerusalem in ruins. Needless to say, the numerous sermons, Bible study

FROM STUCK TO LIMITLESS 115

lessons, and other methods of *renewing my mind* left me with the clear impression that:

1.God was not pleased with the state of His holy temple (my body).
2.God commanded me to stop being a glutton in His Word.
3.God commanded me to repair the damage I had done to His holy temple and its corresponding walls through His Word.
4.God commanded me to properly maintain His holy temple and walls once the damage had been repaired.

Seven months after I started eating and drinking for the glory of God, I lost eighty-nine pounds. In less than a year, I had shed ninety-nine pounds. After that, the Lord put me on a plateau for a full year. The Holy Spirit taught me at that time that plateaus sometimes occur for a spiritual reason. In this instance, I was kept in that position due to my disobedience.

Once the Lord blessed me to lose the weight, I was commanded to write everything He had taught me. I had the audacity to compose a synopsis of what God had done for me on an index card. When I finally asked why I was not losing weight anymore, the Lord reminded me of His Word to me. Miraculously, the weight easily melted off again once I put pen to paper.

Since then, the Lord used me to start a Christian health and fitness ministry to help people all over the world obtain deliverance from eating disorders and obesity. During the twelve-week course, participants always testify about becoming healthier inside first and foremost.

Class often evolves into testimony service as participants share that they no longer take hypertension medication, their A1-C numbers are normal, or they no longer have high cholesterol. Although I know I am not Moses, I praise the Lord for using me as a vessel to set the captives free and lead them out of the Wilderness of Obesity and Eating Disorders into the Promised Land of Healthy and Fit for Life!

Ann Wooten-Taylor

ABOUT ANN WOOTEN-TAYLOR

ANN WOOTEN-TAYLOR IS the founder and C.E.O. of Eating as an Act of Worship Ministries (hereinafter EAW Ministries), which is a non-profit organization dedicated to teaching the biblical principles regarding the body, dieting, exercising, and maintaining a healthy body for the glory of God.

She is the author of the Eating as an Act of Worship book series, and she teaches the twelve-week EAW Ministries Health and Fitness Course. Moreover, Mrs. Taylor writes the EAW Ministries Health and Fitness Column which has been published by The Narrative Matters,

Back2Eden News Magazine, Godlock Magazine, and Kingdom News Today Magazine.

Furthermore, she hosts the Saturday morning EAW Ministries Radio Show on StudioW Buzz in Richmond, VA, Victory 95.3 FM, 100.9 FM, and 1530 AM in Little Rock, AR, and DFW Den Radio Station, which is an internet radio station.

Most recently, Mrs. Taylor became the hostess and executive producer of the Eating as an Act of Worship Ministries Health and Fitness Television Show, which aired on HMS in Houston, Texas on Comcast 17 and AT&T Uverse 99. The show was also livestreamed at www.hmstv.org.

Mrs. Taylor serves as executive producer of the Teens Talk Truth Radio Show as well as a co-host of The Boomerang Radio Show. In January 2018, she and her spouse were featured in Back2Eden News Magazine regarding Eating as an Act of Worship Ministries. Additionally, Ann is a practicing attorney who has been married for 24 years. She and her husband have two children.

Follow Ann on Social Media:

Facebook: https://www.facebook.com/EAWMinistries

Website: https://www.eatingasanactofworshipministries.org/

VERONICA

Esther's life was plagued by insecurity, fear, and shame, and she struggled to maintain her faith while hiding a painful secret. Coping with her past, she presented a false image of herself, grappled with self-doubt, and questioned why God allowed such events to happen. However, Esther eventually broke free from her past, seeking counseling and empowerment, and now coaches others to live boldly and with purpose.

CHAPTER 12
MY FATHER'S TOUCH

AT THE TENDER age of five, when most preschoolers were thinking about their next adventure, or which toy to claim as their own, the first improper touch came. Unfortunately, I was being inappropriately touched by the man known by our small town as Preacher Man or Minister, who happened to be my father.

Sadly, my experience was not an isolated incident but like many other children who have experienced or will experience abuse, it's catastrophic on multiple levels. The trauma was so deep, it's immeasurable; the effects of its totality crossed generational lines.

Picture, if you can, the life of a youthful, pure, and cheerful child being completely upended by an individual whom she solely recognized as "Daddy."

The great protector, provider, and her first male role model. The man who ultimately stained the framework of her self-worth.

I am she!

I remember walking by the sofa, where he sat, late one evening. Something felt wrong. I didn't know why, or what was wrong, but intuitively I sensed something bad was about to happen.

That 'touch', as well as the many episodes of groping and caresses that followed the initial one, eventually morphed into full-blown sexual, mental, and daily physical neglect and abuse.

He started out with a light caress, then he was almost angry. That's when he got rough and lifted me off the ground with one hand, for what felt like an eternity.

Eventually, I landed on my feet as his red, blood-shot eyes aligned with mine, causing my heart to race at the velocity of a bullet train. The intensity of the moment was such that I feared my heart would rupture out of my chest, while my stomach convulsed with enough force to suggest an impending loss of bowel control. The cumulative effect was the gradual erosion of my tender, five-year-old heart, leaving a lingering taste of bitterness from the fragmented pieces.

The daddy who was supposed to love, cherish, and protect me, subsequently ended up tilting the scale and setting in motion a roller-coaster of emotions that would, if not dealt with, surely wreck me.

That night, the light went out in Harlem. That night, the light of my soul went dark. As our gazes met, I immediately lowered my head, focusing on the floor because what I saw in his eyes was evil in its ugliest form.

Fear and confusion seized hold of my mind, so I did what any other child would do; I made a quick beeline to the small room I shared with my sibling.

Over the course of several weeks, and then a few months later, the inappropriate touching and sexual fondling progressed rapidly to full vaginal penetration, accompanied by vulgar insults. Within a few days of the initial contact, I began plotting an escape route. Although it is difficult to comprehend how a five-year-old could understand the gravity of the situation, I can only surmise that it was an innate, intuitive sense. That dreadful night, my childhood innocence perished, and a survivor emerged.

On every occasion that he uttered my name, my heart would palpitate, generating a mixture of aversion and apprehension toward him. Despite my efforts to shun him, living in a compact single wide trailer limited my personal space and seclusion. Consequently, evading encounters with him posed a formidable challenge. I resorted to closely monitoring his daily routine to avoid crossing his path. However, my actions proved futile, as we shared the same space.

Although the exact details of how Mom discovered the situation remain unclear, her strength and courage were undeniable. I can still remember the way she quickly entered our shared bedroom, grabbed something we didn't see, and ran out of the room. The explosion and the scene that met our eyes told us she'd shot our father. Even though he survived, he returned to the house and made empty promises to change his ways, but it was a lie. The abuse escalated.

My mom tried to leave several times, packing us into the car to stay with relatives, but it wasn't long before we were forced to return to our terrifying home environment. On one occasion, she told us she was going to leave us with our father temporarily. I begged her not to leave, fearing for our safety, but thankfully she stayed.

Despite everything, I love and appreciate my mother for doing all she could, with the limited resources she had, to protect us from harm.

Years had come and gone, but I never said a word. I taught myself to endure the pain until the day I was old enough to escape. Mastering the cat-and-mouse game that ensued, I managed to walk out the door at the same time he entered our home. With calculated precision, I timed it just right several times a week. Unfortunately, he found me each time he 'got the itch'.

There are no words to convey how difficult my life had become. It was as if my discernment was at Warp Five, in that I could feel his ugly presence when he crossed the Henry County line. My internal radar proved right 100% of the time.

My father, a self-reliant truck driver, possessed a fleet of trucks, comprising a few 10-wheelers and predominantly international/Kenworth eighteen wheelers. Consequently, he frequently traveled out of the city for one to two weeks each time. His prolonged absence granted me the opportunity to experience a semblance of a regular childhood. As his arrival drew near, an overwhelming apprehension consumed me, reminiscent of a foreboding storm cloud looming over me, penetrating my being to the core.

My anxiety grew during that time—my stomach ached and fear gripped the core of my soul. Once he got home, the cat-and-mouse game started again. I often prayed silently to God—something like, "Lord please don't let the door squeak,"—because in my mind, a non-

FROM STUCK TO LIMITLESS   123

squeaking door meant safety. But time and time again, he found me when he itched. Although he assaulted me several times every month, it felt like every other day.

At the age of seven, no significant changes had occurred, as a result, I eventually came to accept being violated as my normal way of life, understanding it as the lot that God had chosen for me.

However, upon reflection, I cannot say for certain why or how, but I felt a faint glimmer of hope deep within me, a longing for a better life. This hope was profound and stirred the belief that my circumstances were not permanent. Despite the adversity, I had a sense that someday I would find a way to escape.

The following decade of my life was sheer torment, yet I remained silent because I lacked the language to articulate the heinous actions that were being inflicted upon me.

Many birthdays came and went, and not one of them was celebrated with ice cream or cake. Each birthday was simply another day on a hamster wheel of hell.

Fear gripped my heart because I didn't know what the next decade would bring. Even now, I still struggle with how to wrap my head around what was happening to me. I knew it was something bad, but I still didn't have the skill to put it into words.

Keep in mind, it was a different time. A different era. A different world, to be honest. There was no MTV, social media, or gangster rapping at that time, and trust me, for the most part, church folk didn't talk about abuse, or real-life issues. In my day, it was embedded in the heart of most children that they were to be heard and not seen. Children didn't have an opinion or voice.

Thankfully, my parents introduced me to Christ at an early age. I can recall going to Sunday school and hearing the scriptures read that children should obey their parents, but I don't seem to recall anyone mentioning Ephesians 6:4 (New King James Version).

Fathers, do not provoke your children to anger by the way you treat them. Rather, bring them up with the discipline and instructions that comes from the Lord.

• • •

The days became weeks, months, and then years. I was clueless and had no idea of the painful path my life would take—gripped with insecurities, fear, poor self-image, no voice of my own. I was an introvert, an avoider. I behaved erratically, unable to connect, ashamed, as well as unable to thrive. I felt like I had no one to confide in. It was as if this little girl was on her own.

I have a friend whom I admire greatly because she accepted me for who I am and is always cheerful, something I've always yearned for. I didn't spend much time with her because I was afraid she might ask to visit my house, and I felt responsible for protecting her.

Gradually, I realized that it wouldn't be wise to invite her over due to her physical appearance. She had a curvy figure and liked to wear mid-thigh shorts that accentuated her body. I worried about her safety and the possibility of my father making advances toward her, or if she somehow discovered our family's shameful secret. This friend was not one to stand idly by, but rather, she would have fought back and likely disclosed the truth to the entire town, opening the lid on a proverbial Pandora's box.

As the journey continued, I tried to leave my past behind and strive for a better life. However, I found myself caught between maintaining my faith and being dishonest. My mind wavered between the two. I questioned whether I was truly capable of changing my life through faith or if I was deceiving myself.

To distance myself from my shameful past and blend in with others, I started to fabricate stories and present a false image of a typical life. My aim was to keep my secret hidden from others. However, this habit eventually led me to become a compulsive liar, which robbed me of my authenticity and rendered me powerless.

Consequently, I grappled with feelings of self-doubt and low self-esteem, often questioning the reasoning behind the fact that there was no divine intervention and that God would allow such events to happen. Ultimately, these struggles culminated in a profound sense of self-loathing that permeated every aspect of my being.

Despite the odds, I maintained my faith that one day I would break free. I envisioned a life of liberation and continued to trust in the existence of a higher God even as I remained engulfed in darkness. The morning I longed for was not limited to the early hours of the day; I hoped a metaphorical awakening would come.

Then one night, I suddenly felt a sense of freedom, as if the chains that had once bound me were no longer held together by a lock. Although physically restrained, my mind was free from the shackles of negative thought patterns that had held me captive for so long.

The joy I felt was because I had been praying to God for so many years to deliver me and set me free. That night, He turned my mourning into dancing and gave me beauty by ashes.

Success was not immediate but a journey that began for me at fourteen years of age when I stopped my father from raping me. I sought counseling, read self-help books, and surrounded myself with wise and godly individuals who could help me to grow.

Journaling was a significant part of my journey, as it provided a therapeutic outlet for me to express my thoughts without needing to rationalize or accept them. Over time, I integrated God and His word, speaking affirmatively about myself in alignment with my spiritual beliefs. I rejected thoughts or ideas that did not align with these beliefs, allowing me to rewire my brain, renew my thoughts, and change the trajectory of my life.

Today, the once-broken girl, known as Esther, coaches and empowers others to live their lives boldly and with purpose. A very special thanks to all the therapists, friends, family, ministers, coaches, and a few strangers. All of you were instrumental in helping me heal and move forward.

I never want to forget my journey toward healing, so I sometimes reflect on it. Presently, I have a close personal bond with God—the God of Abraham, Isaac, Jacob, and now the God of Veronica. As a result, I am no longer a victim but a triumphant overcomer who receives daily chances to assist thousands of individuals to reclaim their power and become the extraordinary human they were meant to be.

In my capacity as the President of a Florida based 501c3 non-profit organization, and as a recipient of the prestigious 2022 Presidential Lifetime Achievement Award, I have been presented with numerous opportunities to give back and make a positive impact.

I treat the privilege bestowed upon me with great seriousness, and therefore, I am resolute in my commitment to utilize my position and skills to effect substantial positive changes within my community and beyond.

Veronica Nealy-Morris

ABOUT VERONICA NEALY-MORRIS

VERONICA NEALY-MORRIS IS A PUBLISHED AUTHOR, successful entrepreneur, educator, and motivational speaker. She is a dynamic communicator that speaks from her heart to yours with clarity and understanding.

Veronica has an exceptional gift of tansforming her experiences, trials, and tribulations into a journey of encouragement and joy through the word of God. She has written and facilitated many classes on various topics including *Change, The Power of Words, What's your Secret Sauce, The Art of Communication* and *The Effects of Abuse.*

She is the author of two life changing books: *It's A Process* and *My Dreams Revealed*. Additionally, she has created a journal that allows readers to write and capture their own thoughts & dreams called *The Dream Journal*.

Veronica Nealy-Morris is a native Floridian, born in the small town of Clewiston. She is the third of eight children. Veronica began her career as a Respiratory Therapist in Miami and continued working in the medical industry when she relocated to Orlando. Veronica has had a fulfilling career as a medical professional for over thirty years.

She has been acknowledged by The International Center of Excellence and Authenticity, The Turner 12 Project, in addition to being commissioned with a certificate of appointment as-an honorary Admiral in the Texas Seahorse Squadron.

In 2022, Veronica received a Presidential Life Time Achievement Award signed by the 46th President of the United States, Joe Biden. In addition to her success in the medical industry, Veronica is a wise financial investor and holds the position of President/CEO of a 501C3 non-profit organization based on Orlando, Florida.

A graduate of Fortis College, The Institute of Theology & Ministry Training, University of Metaphysics BS, Veronica earned a degree BA in Biblical Studies. In 2011, Veronica left a wonderful company, where she worked as a lead therapist and began walking in the purpose God placed in her heart many years ago.

Veronica took her first step and has not looked back since. She is now living a purpose-filled life of uplifting, empowering, educating, and motivating women & young girls to live in the N.O.W. (Notice Opportunities and Welcome them)

She currently lives in Orlando Florida with her husband Retired Master Sergeant (USAF) Robert L Morris. Together, their life is beyond amazing.

Follow Veronica on Social Media:
https://bit.ly/KISSMinistryVNM

MARIE

If you are struggling with feelings of worthlessness and emptiness, I want you to know that healing and joy are possible. I understand the challenges that come with mental health struggles. It takes courage to acknowledge your pain and seek help, but you can overcome your difficulties and find a sense of purpose and fulfillment.

I also understand what it's like to feel trapped in a cycle of negativity and despair. The weight of those feelings can be overwhelming, and it may seem like there is no way out. But I also know that with time, effort, and support, you can find a path forward.

If you are struggling with suicidal thoughts, please know there is help available. You are not alone, and there are people who care about you and want to support you. Whether it's talking to a trusted friend or family member, reaching out to a mental health professional, or seeking help from a crisis hotline, there are resources available to you.

With commitment and effort, it is possible to find a life filled with purpose, joy, and meaning. I believe in you, and I know you can overcome your struggles and find a brighter tomorrow.

CHAPTER 13
JOY COMES IN THE MORNING

When thou passest through the waters, I will be with thee; and through the rivers; they shall not overflow thee: when thou walkest through the fire, thou shalt not be burned; neither shall the flame kindle upon thee.
Isaiah 43:2 (King James Version)

JOY IS LIKE LOVE, peace, and faith. You don't always feel it, but you *know* it. It's *believing* in God and always trusting in Him that makes the difference.

It doesn't matter what time of the day or night you're in, it's morning somewhere and there is joy. Feel the joy—it's in you!

My life journey has taken me through the fire, up hills, and down valleys, so I didn't always know or feel joy. However, I emerged better. Not flawless. Not perfect. Better!

Although I'm now an Award-winning and Best-selling author, Registered Nurse, and a Coach, I know what it's like to struggle with depression and be SHUT IN—Silently Hurting due to Unresolved Trauma (caused by sexual assault) Internalizing (taking on shame, anger, fear, anxiety, reliving the trauma) Needlessly—because years ago, that struggle was a reality in my life.

FROM STUCK TO LIMITLESS   131

Most children grow up examining the adults around them, whether those in their homes, neighborhood, on television, or social media, and picture in their mind's eyes, whom they'd love to emulate as they develop into adulthood.

Sometimes as they grow, they mimic the occupation of the person they most admire. Oftentimes, by the tween to teen years, they've already envisioned their vocation, even if they don't know all the details or qualifications and skills required to be successful in that field.

From as far back as I can recall, I wanted to be a registered nurse, just like my favorite adult, my Aunt Herma, and impact the lives of others. At the time I hadn't thought or looked past serving at the bedside. I had no knowledge or inkling of a nurse's life beyond that. Due to financial constraints, that dream did not materialize until I relocated to the United States and was in my thirties.

After a few years of studying and working in different areas of the healthcare field, I earned an Associate Nursing degree. I was elated as my hard work and dedication were finally paying off. Boldly, I stepped out of nursing school and after passing my boards, dived into a life-changing experience, the emergency department.

Naturally, my nerves were frayed in the beginning, but with compassionate mentors and leaders, I learned quickly and thrived. My memory bank failed to release the recollection of the first time I cared for a victim of sexual assault. However, as my experience and knowledge multiplied in that area, my personal fight to overcome what had happened to me as an eleven-year-old child, and later in my teens, threatened to suffocate me. As I cared for and guided those victims, I found my calling and the courage to care for myself and heal.

My life began on the Caribbean island of Jamaica. As is the story of most homes then, my single mother and extended family raised me. At the age of eleven, the husband of one of my aunts added me to the list of his victims.

Prior to that, I had no idea he was a pedophile, otherwise, I wouldn't have been in close proximity to him. However, I later learned that incidents similar to what happened to me, and worse, were *normal* throughout the community where we lived. Many adults knew and chose to be silent bystanders.

It's still shocking that people in our communities and families remained silent, instead of taking action to support and protect victims, especially when a child is involved. How could they remain complicit when so many were and are suffering?

For many years it was my shameful little secret. I internalized the burden of shame, guilt, anger, and grief, and with sealed lips, my life continued on the surface.

There were other instances throughout my teenage years—at school and while riding in public transportation—during which males crossed sexual boundaries with me, which piled on more baggage to what I was already carrying. Shame, guilt, anxiety, and fear were my constant companions.

Many days during my adult years, I woke up feeling of empty and worthless. And at night went to bed thinking of the lack of passion and self-worth that consumed me, even as a wife, by then. It got so bad that I began having suicidal thoughts. Although I hadn't developed a plan, the thought haunted with me for some time.

Even though I didn't seek out a therapist or a sexual assault recovery coach, some of the methods I employed to overcome are within their arsenal. Over time, I connected with other people and organizations that care for and support survivors and joined my voice and resources with theirs to help fight to end this madness. And, although it's a long way from ending, progress is being made.

The best part for me now is that I am healed and I can help others do the same. I want this kind of life for everyone! That's why I do the work that I do. God has called me to advocate for and coach victims of sexual assault and my time and effort are dedicated to serving those who are affected by this horrific crime. My mission is to help them gain clarity, reclaim their lives, and become powerful self-advocates.

Initially, I was hesitant to share too much about my life on social media and anywhere in the public realm. However, my deeper truth is that I care way too much about helping those who are SHUT IN, or stuck in a life of hopelessness, to reignite their passion and claim their God-given potential to let fear stop me.

I know how painful it can be when you've lost your focus because your mojo has been derailed by the effects of unresolved trauma or grief and you become marooned and isolated. That's not how you want your life to be. Please know you are not your trauma and you're not alone. You can rewrite the chapters of your life that were ripped out. You are worthy of living to your full God-given potential.

Life is too short to spend it replaying the same story over and over. Satan is a liar. You are enough. You are worthy of happiness and joy.

My life experiences, combined with over twenty-four years of nursing, and research have equipped me with the skills and knowledge to boldly champion this cause.

My Mission or Vocation appeared ingrained in me even as a young child. *I'm going to be a nurse, like Aunt Herma, and help others.*

It's normal to change careers throughout one's lifetime, whether due to layoffs, a change of heart, or just being shoved in another direction. It happens quite often. As we go through life, we are exposed to different endeavors that may cause us to switch our areas of interest. Our learning and experiences offer new opportunities, some of which hadn't even crossed our minds.

When I received the *call* to go into sexual assault recovery coaching, I hesitated. My question to God was, "Why are you moving me from the bedside where I am doing great work with victims and am needed?"

Sexual Assault Nurse Examiners are special and in short supply. The memory of His response is tattooed in my mind. I'd been out taking my usual morning walk and the thought of leaving direct care had been plaguing me for a few days and I'd been praying. As I walked, the Lord spoke to me. "You don't have to serve the victims by being at the bedside."

This was confirmation to me that coaching victims to be powerful self-advocates would be more far-reaching and impactful than limiting myself to the bedside. The stage was set for me to pursue my purpose.

My coaching platform was developed around the span of my career, my role as a Sexual Assault Nurse Examiner, Advocate, and my collaboration with multidisciplinary teams and organizations that work in concert to help victims of sex crimes gain justice and heal.

Through serving others, I uncovered my inner voice and power, shed my SHUT IN garments, and became a powerful self-advocate and a Rape Kit Expert. I discovered my purpose and Vocation to assist victims by introducing them to the resources and techniques that helped transform my life to support them in moving from SHUT IN to Limitless as I have.

You're not your sexual assault or rape. It's something that someone did to you. You're still the amazing person you were before that experience. You may not know or feel it, but you have the power within to become your own powerful self-advocate, instead of becoming emotionally, mentally, spiritually, and physically SHUT-IN.

You don't have to become a SHUT IN and if you are, it's never too late to get help. Scripture says, in Psalms 147:3 (King James Version)

He healeth the broken in heart, And bindeth up their wounds.

The pieces will come back together no matter your circumstances or how heartbroken you may feel. You will heal. Trust in His promises.

Sexual assault is not okay!
Sexual assault is a crime!
Together we can end this madness!
Don't be a silent bystander. Be an active participant.

A part of my journey from SHUT IN/Stuck to Limitless involved being intentional about my daily self-care. However, I've learned and experienced that sometimes even when you do everything right, circumstances outside your control may jump in and derail what you're working to uphold.

The term, "listen to your body it has stories to tell," was manifested in my life from 2021 to 2022—chest pain, shortness of breath, and other—as it seemed at the time—minor inconveniences, and the list goes on.

Signs and symptoms most times that should not be ignored by anyone, and if I'd heard them from a friend or family member, I'd have rushed them to the doctor for a total overall. I neglected to apply that same sense of urgency to myself.

Several months after the signs and symptoms appeared, and after other diagnostic tests either failed to detect the cause or were inconclusive, I went in for a cardiac catheterization.

The cardiologist's words are still ringing in my ears. "Ms. McKenzie, you have three blocked arteries and one is completely blocked."

Although I wasn't shocked, I had expected negative findings. I didn't think anything was abnormal with my heart and I had listened to him, while I awaited my results, heralding to other patients that their tests were negative.

"No blockages," he sang from room to room as the morning wore on. I waited my turn with high expectations that I'd return home and continue with life and work as I had done the previous day, including resuming my deadlift challenge for the month.

I didn't get back to the challenge that day and for several months afterward. No heavy lifting, I was cautioned.

Looking back, I knew something was wrong. My body was shouting, but I ignored the clues. God had been protecting me as I walked around daily doing life. Fast forward to quadruple bypass and my heart and body feel like I've been restored to the proverbial factory setting.

Self-care is a must. You can't pour from an empty cup. Although I'd been practicing self-care diligently over the past few years, I'm more mindful of that now. You don't have to be diagnosed with a medical problem to have one, it may be brewing inside due to family history, not going to the doctor, or doctors only focusing on your chief complaint and not the whole person when you make a visit.

Throughout this experience, I heard God saying, "Girl, you've got more work to do." Caring for myself has provided me with more energy and time to pour into others. To live a more purposeful journey.

Are you taking time for yourself?

When you feel good, you look good, and show up one hundred percent for yourself and others. You are worthy of living a healthy and fulfilled life.

As I take my clients through the journey of recovery from the effects of sexual assault, I share my story, urge them, and provide resources and tips to help them care for themselves—emotionally, mentally, spiritually, and physically—holistically.

My job as a Registered Nurse is more than knowledge and skills meant to treat, educate, and medicate patients suffering from diseases. I enjoy my profession and have incorporated those transitional skills into my coaching and feel that I offer my clients more than just care. I sense that I touch their souls by offering compassionate, authentic, confidential, and safe space to share, heal, and grow into their wholeness.

If you or someone you know is struggling with the effects of unresolved trauma due to sexual assault/rape, reach out for help and support to heal. Like me, you can and are worthy of experiencing joy and fulfillment.

Healing may be a lifelong process, and we may still be hurt from time to time, but the effects will be diminished by the tools and strategies you adopt to work through the trauma. But, rest assured, you have this promise from the Lord:

For I will turn their mourning to joy, Will comfort them, And make them rejoice rather than sorrow. Jeremiah 31:13 (New King James Version).

Are you SHUT IN – Silently Hurting due to Unresolved Trauma (due to sexual assault) Internalizing (reliving the trauma, anger, fear, anxiety) Needlessly?

The road from SHUT IN/Stuck to Limitless is open for you. Take the first step!

Marie McKenzie

ABOUT MARIE MCKENZIE

AWARD-WINNING AND #1 Bestselling Author Marie McKenzie is a Rape Kit Expert, Coach, Advocate, Sexual assault Nurse Examiner, Registered Nurse Educator, and Speaker.

She helps those affected by sexual assault overcome the trauma, and position them as Powerful Self-Advocates instead of becoming emotionally, mentally, spiritually, and physically Shut-In.

Marie's career as a registered nurse spans over twenty-four years and includes emergency nursing, risk management, leadership, forensic nursing, and education. Through her nursing journey, Marie discovered her passion for serving the victims of sexual violence and those who are stuck due to unresolved loss/trauma.

Her memoir, Things That Keep Me Up At Night, is based on her journey from childhood sexual trauma to healing and thriving. This book has helped transform the lives of many victims, and per reports, is being used as a resource in group counseling sessions.

She advocates for survivors through her books, speaking engagements, coaching, and webinars.

Follow Marie on Social Media:

My links: https://linktr.ee/mckenziemariel

PRACTICING MINDFULNESS

Practicing mindfulness is a powerful tool to help you reduce stress, improve focus, and enhance overall well-being.

Here are some tips to help you practice mindfulness:

Set aside time each day

Even just 10-15 minutes of mindfulness practice each day can be beneficial.

Find a quiet space

Choose a quiet space where you can sit comfortably and without distractions.

Practice deep breathing

Deep breathing is a simple yet powerful mindfulness technique that can help you relax and focus.

Focus on the present moment

Mindfulness is about focusing your attention on the present moment, without judgment or distraction.

By incorporating mindfulness practice into your daily routine, you can reduce stress, improve focus, and enhance your overall well-being.

RESOURCES

IF YOU, or anyone you know is struggling with unresolved trauma, please seek help.

In addition to several authors in this book who are trained in various disciplines, the following organizations offer resources that can help you heal, survive, and thrive.

Centers for Disease Control & Prevention (CDC): https://www.cdc.gov/mentalhealth/index.htm
National Sexual Violence Resource Center (NSVRC): https://www.nsvrc.org/
Rape, Abuse & Incest National Network (RAINN): https://www.rainn.org/
Suicide and Crisis Lifeline: *988*
Suicide Prevention Resource Center: https://sprc.org/
The Inner Truth Project: https://innertruthproject.org/
U.S. Department of Veterans Affairs: https://www.va.gov/health/
Victim Services of Central Florida (VSC): https://victimservicecenter.org/

CPSIA information can be obtained
at www.ICGtesting.com
Printed in the USA
JSHW020545220623
43578JS00001B/7